ARCHITECTURE ASIA

arcasia
Architects Regional Council Asia

中国建筑学会
The Architectural Society of China

Journal of the Architects Regional Council Asia (ARCASIA)

Co-Publishers

The Architectural Society of China (ASC)
9 Sanlihe Road, Beijing, China, 100835

Tongji University
1239 Siping Road, Shanghai, China, 200092

Sponsor

Tongji Architectural Design (Group) Co., Ltd.
1230 Siping Road, Shanghai, China, 200092

Contents

Editorial

In the 21st century, Asia has developed fast in the wave of globalization, and the living and urban environments are changing rapidly along with the economic development. Many Asian cities are undergoing large-scale urban infrastructure construction in the process of rapid urbanization, and a large number of huge iconic buildings representing the characteristics of the country or city have been built. While large-scale construction improves urban conditions, it also results in the redistribution of resources, the occupation of land leading to displacement, and conflicting or unbalanced interests. These are the issues that architects have to face. Alongside this, the development of mobile internet and self-media has also changed the way people present themselves and understand the outside world in the 21st century; this has also enriched the methods of displaying and promoting architecture.

Asia's transition from the 20th to the 21st century has been different from that seen in Europe and the United States. East Asia, Central Asia, South Asia, and Inner Asia have undergone varied experiences and present complex scenarios within each. Even so, some problems are common to certain regions. The research articles in this issue address three different perspectives and dimensions:

1. Public cultural life and space—the transformation of the political space of 1950s China into the cultural space of the 21st century, and how it is used by the public, as well as the type of unresolvable problems and contradictions this change brings is what Charlie Qiuli Xue and his co-authors highlight and reveal.
2. Urban poor housing and social problems—the rapid development of urban infrastructure, its occupation of land, and the resulting displacement of the urban poor are problems many Asian countries encounter in their 21st-century development. Shantanu Khandkar's article addresses these issues, showing how resettlement needs to be seen as an integral part of infrastructure projects and not just as an obstacle to overcome.
3. "Architecture of the self-media age"—the virtual space of the internet has brought about a new way of evaluating architecture, which, unlike the professional, elite discussions of 20th-century architecture, involves ordinary people in the discussion. Sui Yingda and Liu Yanjie's article suggests that the profession should stay aware and critical of this "architecture of the self-media age" by analyzing "Instafamous architecture."

In this issue, we highlight perspectives on the transformation of spatial functions, the contradiction between urban development and individual dwellings, and architecture in the age of self-media, to discuss Asian architecture in the 21st century, hoping to shed light on the different situations and provoke reflection. The projects in this issue provide a response to the complex transformations facing Asian architecture and cities in the 21st century through three aspects: the shaping of the environment from child care to spiritual sanctuary reflects the transformation of user needs from "material" to "spiritual" in the new era; the functional development from temporary exhibition to conference and exposition demonstrates the increasing richness of citizens' public life; and the spatial migration from the urban fringe to the countryside reflects the local transformation in the urban development trend.

Cultural Megastructures and Chinese Cities in the 21st Century: The Case of the Grand Theater

Charlie Qiuli XUE, City University of Hong Kong, China
ZHANG Lujia, City University of Hong Kong, China
SUN Cong, City University of Hong Kong, China
Gianni TALAMINI, City University of Hong Kong, China

Abstract

The 21st century has seen an unprecedented urban construction wave in China, during which more than 400 grand theaters have been erected. The number of theaters in China that have been either newly built or renovated over the last two decades surpasses the total number of theaters that have been constructed in Western countries since the end of World War II. This study examines the production of cultural megastructures in China and identifies the motivations behind this production. Any increase in material wealth is usually accompanied by a demand for high-quality cultural consumption, and the desire to enhance a city's status spurs on the production of artistic spaces and glamorous landmarks. These motivations make cultural megastructures both an arena for international architects and a gentrified space for the city' elite. This article queries and discusses the performance of grand theaters in cities, with the goal of establishing a more effective way of evaluating public cultural buildings. The authors hope to make a case for a more justifiable and accessible usage of public cultural buildings to serve the majority of people.

Keywords

Cultural buildings, megastructures, grand theaters, Chinese cities, design.

Author Information
Charlie Qiuli XUE: bscqx@cityu.edu.hk, ORCiD: 0000-0003-4835-7458
ZHANG Lujia: lujzhang2-c@my.cityu.edu.hk, ORCiD: 0000-0002-9379-9549
SUN Cong (corresponding author): cong.sun@my.cityu.edu.hk, ORCiD: 0000-0001-7439-5533
Gianni TALAMINI: gianntal@cityu.edu.hk, ORCiD: 0000-0003-1480-5267

Figure 1
People's Auditorium: (left) Chongqing, 1954; (right) Wuhan, 1959

1. Introduction

The turn of the 21st century split post-Mao China into two equal periods making up two decades each. In the first period, the country reformed its socialist economic infrastructure and embraced the market economy; in the new millennium, China navigated the ocean of globalization and enjoyed high-speed development. At the beginning of the 1980s, provincial and municipal governments faced a widespread scarcity of buildings, urban facilities, and infrastructure, in terms of both quantity and quality. This included cultural buildings. The auditoriums and Great Halls of People built during the socialist period of the planned economy were not technically adequate to the needs of international musicians and performances.

In 1998, a grand theater designed by the French architectural firm Jean-Marie Charpentier was completed in Shanghai's People's Square. It was arguably the first cultural building in China to result from an international design competition. Since then, there has been a proliferation of grand theaters in Chinese cities of various tiers, alongside museums, libraries, and cultural palaces. In the first two decades of the 21st century, 450 grand theaters and 5,000 museums were erected or renovated. The typical Chinese grand theater of the 21st century usually contains two or more performance halls, with a concert hall, an opera house, or sometimes a minor experimental (box) theater. Cultural megastructures have blossomed concurrently in old cities and new towns.

What forces motivated the production of these cultural megastructures? Can these cultural buildings improve the quality of urban spaces and people's lives? Billions of dollars have been spent by the government and by corporations on cultural buildings. Sporadic reports have lauded these buildings' glamour, but few have engaged seriously with the above questions. This article aims to shed new light on the recent Chinese wave of cultural buildings by reviewing the design trends critically and investigating their effects. It aims to add to our understanding of China's modern architectural history by providing valuable insight into the design practice surrounding contemporary cultural buildings.

2. Cultural Megastructures and the City

In terms of building scale, the grand theaters in China can be categorized as megastructures, a term that was first defined by renowned architect, Fumihiko Maki, in the 1960s as follows: "A large frame in which all the functions of a city or part of a city are housed. It has been made possible by present-day technology. In a sense, it is a manmade feature of the landscape."[1] Kenzō Tange defined megastructures as a mass human-scale form consisting of a mega-form and discrete, rapidly changing functional units within a broad framework.[2] Kenneth Frampton, architect and author, proposed that the megastructure (mega-form) is an urban spatial intervention analogous to an urban landscape and a landmark. Mega-forms (usually horizontally extended) can cure a city's illness like "urban acupuncture." European urban design (renewal) cases were cited in Frampton's theoretical work.[3]

Many recent projects can be seen as megastructures, including conference centers, grand theaters, super high-rise landmark buildings, universities, airport terminals, and other infrastructural complexes. Megastructures often stand for the rights and power of rulers/owners, the prosperity of regions or countries, and the advancement of construction technology. Moreover, the impact of megastructures on the urban spatial structure can change the urban geography, way of life, and economy.[4] Therefore, cultural megastructures are not merely giant cultural buildings.

In this article, a cultural megastructure is understood as a cultural building or cultural cluster, the production of which is governmentally led and the size of which impacts the urban landscape and city image. In the 21st century, Chinese cities tend to rely on such cultural megastructures to shape the space and image of their new districts and to reflect their aspirations.

Performance and exhibition buildings have long been used as social venues and demonstrations of community strength. They have usually been more prominent than other buildings and were the prototypical "mega-forms" of their era, such as Palais Garnier (Garnier Opera House) in Paris, which was completed in 1875, and the buildings constructed for the World's Columbian Exposition in Chicago, which was held in 1893. In some cases, these cultural megastructures can contribute significantly to reshaping an urban area and the image of a city. The Lincoln Center in New York City (with three theaters), which was built in the 1950s, together with more than seventy museums, theaters, and libraries, changed New York from a financial hub into a cultural metropolis. With its unique white-shell cladding, the Sydney Opera House has been the city's pride, as well as its symbol, since its completion in 1973.[5]

In the 1980s, the "presidential projects" of Paris,[6] with the newly renovated Louvre, the Bastille Opera House, the national library, and other museums made the historic city shine again within Europe.[7] In the 1990s, the Guggenheim Museum Bilbao in Bilbao, Basque Country, Spain, awakened the once-deserted Spanish industrial town and brought more than one million tourists annually to this town of 250,000 residents, creating the coined term, the "Guggenheim effect." The high cost of building was compensated for by revenues from tourists from all over the world.[8] Bilbao set a new worldwide model for culturally led urban renewal, triggered by a cultural megastructure. At the beginning of the 21st century, Singapore and Seoul implemented that model on the grounds that a "global city for the arts" can create a "saleable tourism product," while providing an "environment for living and working."[9] International architects designed several cultural megastructures for the two cities.[10]

Throughout the 20th century, cultural and theatrical structures, and later cultural megastructures, were built as a civic celebration of the arts and for the purpose of city branding.[11] The management of Chinese cities observed and admired this model and placed it on their agenda for implementation.

3. The Motivation Behind Chinese Cultural Megastructures

3.1 The Demand for Cultural Venues and Consumption

Art was an indispensable part of civic life at the time when Chinese cities entered modernity. In the eyes of the Communist Party, "art is a powerful weapon for uniting people, educating people, and beating the enemy."[12] In the Communist fortress of Yan'an, during the anti-Japanese war (1938–1946), an auditorium with a wooden structure was built and revolutionary plays were staged there to motivate cadres and boost morale. Multifunctional auditoriums were erected sporadically during the 1950s (Figure 1). When the economy eventually came to allow, the auditorium would later be built on a large scale; conversely, smaller-scale buildings were constructed during stringent times, employing simple technology. These auditoriums were mainly used for political assemblies, education, and motivating people; a typical example is the Shanghai Culture Square, which was completed in 1956. A greyhound racing course built in the 1920s was renovated and converted into a semi-open structure capable of accommodating 15,000 people. Though gambling was forbidden by the Communist government, the ample space that was once the racecourse could be reused.

When China embarked on economic reform and the market economy replaced the planned economy, political gatherings gave way to cultural consumption. The "class struggle" was abandoned and the government focused on the "four modernizations" and how to improve dilapidated cities and people's lives. In 1995, the State Council announced that government departments and state-owned institutions would implement a five-day workweek system. Many joint ventures and private firms followed this practice, which liberated urban dwellers somewhat from work constraints and allowed time for cultural consumption. Subsequently, a significant portion of the urban population obtained sufficient leisure time to enjoy their lives and pursue culture and education; the cultural industry began to attract more patronage. The middle-class marked its particular taste through its distinctive choice of cultural products, forming distinction and distance from other societal strata.[13]

In the following year, the Ministry of Culture announced the nationwide construction of more than fifty cultural facilities, such as libraries, museums, and theaters "compatible with the economic level of and representing the image of the state and relevant cities."[14] The spectacle- and consumption-based economies were fed by a generation of "new needs" to increase people's expenditure; an audience was nurtured to consume leisure activities and cultural events. As noted by Sharon Zukin, professor of sociology, "When cities are dominated by the service economy, aesthetics play an important role in the use of space and lifestyles."[15]

The massive cultural consumption stimulated cultural production and the building of facilities for cultural purposes. Some theaters were born during this wave of construction. For example, the Shanghai International Dance Center consolidated several dancing troupes and planned a rehearsal base, performance venue, and school in the west part of Shanghai. The city organized a series of international dance competitions on account of this new facility.

This cultural venue construction wave also saw to the needs of the Shanghai Symphony Orchestra. This first philharmonic orchestra in China was set up in the Shanghai International Settlement in early 1922. However, they did not have a decent venue for practicing or recording—for example, the air conditioning had to be turned off, even in the hot summer months, to prevent noise interference while recording. In 2009, the Shanghai government allocated the 1950s Shanghai diving pool plot to the orchestra. The site is located in the old French Concession, over Metro Line 10, which passes underground. Facing this challenge, the Japanese acoustic consultant Yasuhisa Toyota, famous for the design of Suntory Hall, a concert hall in Tokyo, and Disneyland in Los Angeles, was invited to design the auditorium. An architectural design competition was held, and a team consisting of the Japanese architect Arata Isozaki and Tongji Architectural Design (Group) Co., Ltd. won out of four competitors (Figure 2).

Figure 2
Concert Hall, Shanghai Symphony Orchestra, Shanghai, 2013; designed by Arata Isozaki and Tongji Architectural Design (Group) Co., Ltd.

In 2013, the Shanghai Symphony Orchestra secured a new home near the opera house of the Shanghai Conservatory of Music; designed by the French architect Christian de Portzamparc, it was completed in 2019. The area serves established and emerging musicians with a music hall and has an opera house that accommodates rehearsals, performances, and tours of international troupes.

Shanghai has a population of twenty-four million and is the richest city in China; its GDP per capita was about US$23,000 in 2020.[16] The city's large and well-established middle-class is able to afford plenty of entertainment consumption over and above meeting its material living costs. However, the number of theaters and seats in Shanghai is still lower than that in London.[17] Building grand theaters can help the city to restore its historic glory, revitalize urban districts, and satisfy the increasing societal demand for culture.

First-tier cities like Shanghai were anxious to build decent theaters to meet the high demand for the arts in the 1990s. Concurrently, second-tier cities felt an even more significant lack of public and entertainment buildings. In China, more than half of urban dwellers live in second- or third-tier cities. Zhengzhou, the provincial capital of Henan Province, historically enjoyed locational advantages as a railway junction in central China. At the beginning of the 21st century, its population of 2.5 million was concentrated within the old urban area of about 132 square kilometers, with a few worker's clubs built in the 1950s. When Japanese master Kisho Kurokawa planned the 150-square-kilometer Zhengdong New District in 2001, a cultural center and a convention center were first set up to anchor the new waterfront hub. The circular artificial reconstructed lake is a symbolic dragon head, surrounded by two rings of high-rise residential and office buildings. The dragon extends its tail six kilometers northward—which encompasses numerous commercial and residential properties. The Henan Art Center within the district was designed by PPA Architects, in cooperation with the design institute of AVIC (Aviation Industry Corporation of China) (Figure 3). It contains a 1,860-seat multipurpose theater, an 800-seat concert hall, a 300-seat black box theater, and a fine arts gallery. With its brand-new cultural facilities, Zhengdong New District became a paradise for the city's middle-class and housing prices in the area rose sharply. Both inside and outside the cultural center, especially on its platform facing the lake, people can be seen strolling, sitting, chatting, and passing their evenings and weekends. From 2010 to 2020, the theaters in the Henan Art Center staged between 200 to 400 performances a year, and over 450 in 2019 alone.[18] This number is close to that of Beijing and Shanghai.

In 2020, the Zhengzhou Grand Theater was opened to the public. Located on the west side of the city, the new theater is part of a newly built cultural cluster called the Central Cultural District (Zhengzhou Cultural District). Popular modern Chinese dramas, famous Broadway musicals, classical ballets, and symphony orchestra performances are staged in this second-tier city. These cultural facilities enrich urban cultural life, as is reflected by the growing number and quality of performances and the rising takings of the box office.

Despite the fast improvements, culturally driven urban development remains in its infancy. Most grand theaters can only obtain subsidies from the provincial government, and the total amount available for expenditure is kept unchanged. Without extra subsidies, Chinese grand theaters cannot

Figure 3
Henan Art Center, 2009; designed by PPA Architects, in collaboration with AVIC's design institute

afford famous worldwide performing groups or expensive projects. At the same time, the gap between ticket prices and what is affordable for consumers remains significant. Policies are still required to motivate the market in second-tier cities. In 2007, the average number of professional theaters per million people in the United States, Germany, the United Kingdom, France, and Japan was 1.8, 3.4, 4.0, 4.2, and 4.4, respectively; in contrast, China had only 0.64 theaters per million people in 2013. In 2018, this number in China was still less than 1 per million people.[19] When considering the uneven distribution of cultural resources, the second- or lower-tier cities enjoy even smaller shares.

During the National government (1927 to 1949), Nanjing was China's capital city, but after 1949 it was simply the provincial capital of Jiangsu Province. Despite its splendid ancient and modern history, the city is not superior to other provincial cities. This took a turn after the completion of The Jiangsu Grand Theater in 2017. Since then, the number of performances held in the theater have been increasing annually, with more public, non-profit-making, and self-made programs and high-end shows (Figure 4). Even in the pandemic situation of 2020, the Jiangsu Grand Theater staged 650 shows, setting a record for China, and arguably, for the world. Before the building of the grand theater, Nanjing's primary performances needed to be held in the National Hall, which was completed in 1936.

As provincial capitals, Zhengzhou and Nanjing share the status of being both provincial and municipal cities. In Zhengzhou, the Henan Art Center (provincial) in the east part and the Zhengzhou Grand Theater (municipal) in the west part add considerable seating capacity to this city in central China. Cultural resources become concentrated in this kind of provincial city. Similar examples are to be found in Nanjing, Hangzhou, Guangzhou, Wuhan, and Chengdu, which also benefit from double public spending.

3.2 City-Branding Ambitions

Theaters often play a crucial role in city branding and have the potential to shape new urban images. In the fierce economic competition among cities, many second-tier Chinese cities like Zhengzhou and Nanjing are planning new cultural and administrative centers, which will need grand theaters, museums, libraries, and art galleries.

Globalization removes barriers between countries and allows for faster circulation of goods, people, and capital. Over the past thirty years, globalization has shaped both urbanization and urban development;[20] urbanization speeds up the global economy. Space and location are increasingly losing their significance, and every city possesses the potential to be an economic and cultural hub. Cities in China inevitably wish to join the global competition by establishing and promoting/marketing their own urban images;[21] this competition has quickly changed the face of Chinese cities.

There is a close relationship between the use of space, city marketing, and image-making. Local authorities are increasingly concerned with establishing an attractive urban image and promoting their city (place marketing) to other countries or regions.[22] Like libraries, museums, and grand theaters, high-class cultural facilities are solid evidence of a pleasant urban environment in regional and global competition. The government expects that when the hardware of a city (for example, infrastructure, cultural buildings, and housing) has been

Figure 4
Jiangsu Grand Theater, 2019, designed by East China Architectural Design Institute; team led by Cui Zhongfang

prepared, there will be natural inflows of money and brains to power the economy. Therefore, Chinese cities at the central and provincial levels tend to chase after "being connected with the international track."[23] In other words, the government sets the goal of building an international image for the city by applying international principles. In 2005, more than 400 cities vowed to become "international metropolises."[24] A direct and straightforward way to achieve this is to take as role models, one's successful neighbor cities or countries.

After two decades of economic reform and wealth accumulation, Chinese cities started to erect flagship cultural projects—libraries, grand theaters, and museums—to enhance their global reputation and compete within China and globally. This trend began in the late 1990s. Culture is the best indicator of prosperity and metropolitan glamour and is a way of "defining a rich, shared identity and thus engender pride of place."[25] Culture is looked to as the key to saving cities from recession in the manufacturing industries, acting as a remedy and savior. Shanghai, Tianjin, and Zhengzhou have all looked to culture as a solution to their problems. A strategic paper for London states that "culture is a strong force [in] promot[ing] understanding and forming the city's identities. It can transcend obstacles and gather people from different backgrounds. Culture can stimulate inspiration, bring education, and create fortune and endless pleasures."[26]

Cultural competence is formalized in cities' development plans. In the *13th Five-year Plan for Shanghai's Economic and Social Development* issued in 2016, for example, "Enhancing Cultural Soft Power" stands as a chapter all in its own. Regarded as a significant means of raising the cohesion and "core" competitiveness of a city, cultural soft power should be strengthened through the full utilization of key facilities, events, and leading master artists. To build "an international cultural metropolis," Shanghai has launched a group of related policies to integrate culture, economy, and society. The *World Cities Culture Report* was first issued in 2011 by London, New York, Tokyo, and Paris, who worked together to produce the report; an up-to-date version is published every year. More than sixty indicators are recorded for each city, including the number of performing arts venues and total seats.[27]

To achieve the goal of becoming an "international cultural metropolis," cultural facility projects are in high demand, both in terms of quantity and quality, and tend to be built at strategic locations to either consolidate the old city or anchor and orient the new districts. Shanghai is not alone in this. As set out in the *Ninth Five-Year Plan (1996–2000)*, the planning of cultural business is led by the Ministry of Culture, which expects first- to fourth-tier cities to boost their cultural industry. As cultural flagships' obvious catalytic function, district governments are enthusiastically grabbing landmark projects within their areas of administration. Many cultural megastructures are built on the strength of hasty decisions with little consultation. In our investigation, most grand theaters need various forms of government sponsorship. Only a few—such as the National Center for the Performing Arts in Beijing and the Shanghai Oriental Art Center—can survive on their own in the market.

As a cultural flagship project, grand theaters function both as art venues and as abstract symbols of the city. To be able to hold multiple types of performances in one building, a grand theater should be able to satisfy several conditions, such as offering a comfortable auditorium, a clear sightline and

Figure 5
The symbolizations of a grand theater: (top to bottom) Beijing National Center for the Performing Arts; Shanghai Grand Theater; Fuzhou Strait Culture and Art Center; Wuxi Grand Theater

City	Number of grand theaters	Examples (Where available, the number of fans in the theater's official Weibo site is included within brackets to indicate its popularity)	Ranking of GDP in China, 2020
Shanghai	9	Shanghai Grand Theater (640,000), Shanghai Oriental Art Center (33,292), Shanghai Culture Square (75,473), Shanghai Poly Grand Theater (14,775), Concert Hall, Shanghai Symphony Orchestra (53,380), Wanping Theater, Fengxian Forest Theaters (1,081), Opera, Shanghai Conservatory of Music (25,975), Shanghai Grand Opera	1
Shenzhen	6	Shenzhen Culture Center (27,181), Shenzhen Poly Grand Theater (18,972), Arts Center of Baoan, Shenzhen Grand Opera, Pingshan Cultural Center, Banxuegang Art Center	3
Beijing	5	National Center for the Performing Arts (2,430,000), Beijing Tianqiao Performing Arts Center (32,654), Beijing Poly Theater, Beijing Cultural Granary Theater, China Philharmonic Hall	2
Chongqing	4	Chongqing Grand Theater (18,556), Chongqing Guotai Art Center (3,845), Chongqing Bishan Cultural and Art Center, Sanxia Art Center	5
Hangzhou	4	Hangzhou Grand Theater (53,578), Hangzhou Yuhang Opera (5,947), The Grand Theater and Concert Hall of Zhejiang Conservatory of Music, Hangzhou Yunhe Grand Theater	8
Suzhou	3	Suzhou Culture and Arts Center (17,261), Wuzhong Public Cultural Center, Suzhou Bay Cultural Center (183)	6
Guangzhou	3	Guangzhou Opera House (880,000), Sunac Guangzhou Grand Theater, Xinghai Music Hall (29,959)	4
Chengdu	2	Sichuan Grand Theater (8,657), Chengdu City Concert Hall (13,116)	7
Nanjing	2	Jiangsu Center for the Performing Arts (52,480), Nanjing Poly Grand Theater (57,800)	10

Table 1
Chinese cities that have constructed the largest number of grand theaters since the 2000s

good acoustic effects, and advanced mechanical and automatic stage facilities. On top of that, with status as an iconic building, both the government and the residents have expectations for a grand theater from a cultural stand; it should symbolize the local identity and serve as a progressive gesture. In a news report on the proposal for the Henan Art Center, local media claimed that "cultural facilities are venues for carrying out cultural activities and enhancing people's cultural education. They are necessary for international cultural exchange and stand as important symbols of the city's cultural development and taste."[28]

To satisfy the residents' collective image of a grand theater, architects frequently apply the double-skin design strategy, which involves creating a shoebox concert hall to meet the performance requirements and an outer skin wrapping the shoebox, which forms the lobby and the auxiliary spaces. The external skin is often shaped plastically to cater to the perception of "resembling something" legendary. For instance, in Beijing's National Center for the Performing Arts (also known as the National Grand Theater), the three auditoriums have independent roofing systems, with and an oval titanium shell that covers them. The shining shell has been lauded as "an opening curtain." The Shanghai Oriental Art Center was designed in the shape of "five magnolia petals" (symbolically referring to Shanghai's city flower) wrapped around three performance spaces. The Hangzhou Grand Theater stands as a "bright crescent moon playing like a jewel on the West Lake." The Henan Art Center symbolizes "dinosaur eggs and ancient musical instruments." Guangzhou Opera House carries the meaning of "two pebbles on the bank of the Pearl River." The Chongqing Grand Theater is designed as a "vessel plowing the water" and as a "tank." The Wuxi Grand Theater symbolizes a "butterfly" and the Wuzhen Theater, a "double lotus." Most of these theaters overlook the waterfront, where their reflections on the water create awesome, crystalline, and flawless icons. For example, the latest theater projects—the Zhuhai Grand Theater, Fuzhou Strait Culture and Art Center, Shanghai Poly Grand Theater, and the Nine Tree Art Center in Fengxian (also known as Fengxian Forest Theaters)—were all built on waterfront sites (Figure 5).[29]

Because of the unusual form and decorative features, these cultural buildings are so "high" (cost and maintenance wise) as to sometimes be beyond their cities' fiscal means. Toward the end of the 1980s, the Shenzhen municipal government spent almost all of its budget building eight cultural facilities. At the beginning of the 21st century, Shanghai also faced financial stresses in building its grand theater. As they represent political achievements, these cultural projects took priority over all others. Therefore, the government determinedly allocated any available financial, material, and workforce resources to their construction.

Roy and Ong wrote about this phenomenon and approach to policy in China and elsewhere in Asia:

> Caught in the vectors of particular histories, national aspirations, and flows of cultures, cities have always been the principal sites for launching world-conjuring projects. Urban dreams and schemes play with accelerating opportunities and accidents that circulate in ever-widening spirals. Emerging nations exercise their new power by assembling glass and steel towers to project particular visions of the world.[30]

Skyscrapers, grand theaters, and other cultural buildings in Chinese cities are among these "world-conjuring projects." Roy and Ong see this as a situation specific to Asia: "Urban dwellers in Asia's big cities do not read spectacles as a

Figure 6
(Left) National Taichung Theater; (right) National Kaohsiung Center for the Arts – both theaters provide ample interior space for public activities

generalized aesthetic effect of capitalism, but rather as symbols of their metropolis that invite inevitable comparison with rival cities."[31] However, in our argument, middle-class urban dwellers in China, and elsewhere in Asia, read these spectacles both as an aesthetic effect of increasing consumerism and as a point of pride in the competition with rival cities. Many second-tier cities do not build as many skyscrapers as first-tier cities but emphasize the role of cultural megastructures instead.

In China, the cultural industry, together with cultural accumulation (historical heritage), cultural management, cultural potential, and cultural exchanges, are factors in assessing a city's cultural competitiveness.[32] In the national ranking of Chinese cities on cultural competitiveness, Beijing, Shanghai, Guangzhou, Hangzhou, and Nanjing are listed as the top five. This is also compatible with their ranking in GDP per capita. The quantity and quality of newly built grand theaters may also reflect this tendency. Table 1 shows the number of newly built grand theaters in some cities. However, the number in theaters may not reflect the whole picture. The number of fans in the theaters' official Weibo page may only partially reflect the theaters' popularity. The grand theaters in Beijing, Guangzhou, and Shanghai enjoy the largest audience pools.

In sharp contrast with China's production of cultural megastructures, cities in other countries are not investing in the construction of grand theaters. The most recent theater complex in New York City is the Lincoln Center, which was built in the late 1960s, with an extension added in the 2000s. The major theaters and concert halls in London were built in the 1950s and 1960s, and the Royal Opera's renovation took place in the early 1990s. The presidential projects in Paris were primarily completed in the 1980s. In the relay race to build grand theaters, the baton was passed to China in the 21st century, and the production of cultural megastructures accelerated.

4. The Problems Associated with Grand Theaters

Thousands of cultural megastructures, including more than 400 grand theaters, are scattered across various first-, second-, and third-tier Chinese cities. The investment in a grand theater building in the 21st century is generally around RMB one billion (approximately US$160 million in 2018). Most theaters rely on government subsidies, box office incomes, and multiple commercial side-operations to maintain profitable status. These cultural buildings have consolidated Chinese cities' status in the region, province, and world. The question is, have they enhanced the cities' branding and improved people's cultural lives as expected? For the question of city branding, a reliable measurement must be established. An extended period of observation is needed to answer the question concerned with enhancing people's quality of life. Here, we present and discuss preliminary findings from our observation over the last decade.

4.1 Far Away From Ordinary Residents

As most grand theaters and cultural buildings are built for city branding and place marketing, their icons/images are central in their production. Most buildings are located in the center of the new town, far away from the historically consolidated urban areas where most residents live. Some grand theaters were built on the waterfront of natural or artificial lakes, for example, those in Zhuhai, Wuxi, Fuzhou, and Changsha. These are far-flung locations

Figure 7
Two grand theaters designed by gmp: (left) Chongqing Grand Theater, 2009; (right) Qingdao Grand Theater, 2011

that are difficult to reach from the central areas of the city. It takes an hour and a half by public transportation from Wuxi's old city to reach the Wuxi Grand Theater, which is located on the shoreline of Taihu Lake. The Meixi Lake Cultural and Art Center in Changsha stands on former agricultural land. The front lake, which produces the reflection in the water, was dug specifically for the theater. The people of Changsha would prefer to gather in the city's cultural center than take a thirty-minute subway ride to Meixi Lake. The nearest subway station to Shanghai's Poly Grand Theater is 2.2 kilometers away from the theater, without a proper last-mile public transportation connection.

According to Frampton, mega-forms should cure the city's illness through their diverse types of connectivity, much like acupuncture. However, the Chinese cultural megastructures are mostly "sculptures" on the lawn that look impressive at a distance. They are more monuments than connectors and containers of civic activities.

4.2 The Exclusive "Public" Space

In the designs of all the new grand theaters we looked at in our investigation, consideration is given to providing ample indoor and outdoor space for public activities. The lobbies are usually fabulously designed, with flowing high-low spaces, curtain walls, and high-class cladding on the walls and floors. However, most of these indoor spaces are only open to ticket holders for an hour before the performance.

The Shanghai Grand Theater often appears in postcards and tourist information leaflets. Unfortunately, however, the outdoor grassland is always protected with a fence. Passers-by can only appreciate the crystalline, sculpture-like theater from a distance. Many residents in the surrounding areas have never had a chance to enter the theater. The management has explained that it would increase the management's cost and risk if they removed the fence and opened the lobby. There would be countless people and tourist buses occupying the front square and damaging the pavement, and once people flood into the lobby, the situation could become difficult to manage.[33] In Tianjin, the grand theater overlooking the waterfront seldom opens its lobby, unless for important celebratory events. Even on performance days, audience members can only enter from the side door, with no chance of experiencing the grand gate facing the waterfront.

One of the few positive examples contradicting such public barring is seen in the Shanghai Symphony Orchestra Concert Hall. The lobby and exhibition gallery, where musical instruments and interactive sound devices are displayed, are open to the public. In a similar vein, the Shanghai Grand Theater is located in the historic French Concession area, surrounded by lively, harmonious, and intimate street life. In the Suzhou Culture and Art Center as well, the lobby is open, owing to the art gallery, cinema, and theater sharing the same lobby. However, the thousands of square meters of floor space in the lobby appear empty to the visitor as the space is inadequately used.

Even if so, requesting theaters to have a freely accessible lobby may still be asking too much. Libraries are born to be open to the public, whereas theaters are not. According to our observations, the theaters in New York, Toronto, Barcelona, Madrid, Stockholm, and Paris do not open their lobbies outside of performances. Only the theaters in London, Oslo, Hong Kong, and Taiwan are found to welcome the public to use their lobbies—which have cafes, restaurants, exhibitions, and toilet facilities—

Schematic designer	Name of theater	City	Completion year	Brief introduction
gmp, Germany	Chongqing Grand Theater	Chongqing	2009	Concert hall and opera house, a total of 2,770 seats; on the junction of two rivers
	Tianjin Grand Theater	Tianjin	2012	4 halls, a total of 3,121 seats; standing with a library, an art gallery, and a history museum
	Qingdao Grand Theater	Qingdao	2009	3 halls, a total of 3,258 seats; located between the mountains and the sea
	Guangxi Art and Cultural Center	Nanning	2017	3 halls, with 3,600 seats
	Langfang Grand Theater	Langfang	2019	3 halls, with 3,300 seats
	Chengdu City Concert Hall	Chengdu	2019	4 halls, with 3,400 seats
Carlos Ott, Canada	Hangzhou Grand Theater	Hangzhou	2004	3 halls, with 2,600 seats
	Dongguan Yulan Grand Theater	Dongguan	2005	2 halls, with 2,000 seats
	Henan Arts Center	Zhengzhou	2008	3 halls, with 3,004 seats; together with an art museum
	Wenzhou Grand Theater	Wenzhou	2009	3 halls, with 2,239 seats
	Shenlong Grand Theater	Zhuzhou	2016	2 halls, with 1,737 seats
Paul Andreu, France	National Performing Arts Center	Beijing	2007	4 halls, a total of 5,850 seats; covered in a single egg-shaped roof
	Suzhou Cultural and Arts Center	Suzhou	2006	2 halls, with 1,672 seats; together with an art gallery and cinemas
	Oriental Arts Center	Shanghai	2005	A concert hall, an opera house, and a recital hall hosted in a five-petal magnolia shape
	Shandong Grand Theater	Jinan	2012	3 halls, with 3,729 seats; building mass spread like the petal of a flower
Arata Isozaki, Japan	Shenzhen Concert Hall	Shenzhen	2007	2 halls, with 2,183 seats; together with a library
	Shanghai Symphony Orchestra Concert Hall	Shanghai	2013	A 2,000-seat concert hall and a 300-seat recital hall
	Harbin Concert Hall	Harbin	2017	2 halls, with 1,600 seats
	Datong Grand Theater	Datong, Shanxi	2018	2 halls, with 2,300 seats

Table 2
Foreign firms that are the most successful in designing grand theaters in China

during the daytime. These theaters include the Festival Hall and the Royal Opera in London; the Cultural Center, the City Hall, and the regional town halls in Hong Kong; the National Taichung Theater (an opera house); and the National Kaohsiung Center for the Arts (a performing arts center) (Figure 6). Theater lobbies in these cities are always hustling and bustling. The pyramid of the Oslo Opera House, too, famously invites many people to climb it. These lobbies give warmth and a sense of the muse within to ordinary citizens and visitors who do not have an admission ticket, and thus these cultural buildings display the spirit of the public place. Given the enormous investment they require, the magnificent space they occupy, the prominent status they have in the city, and the citizens' high expectations of them, Chinese theaters' social functions need to be on full display, and the public funding they receive should be better justified.

4.3 International Arena or a Lesson for Chinese Architects?

Since an open-door policy was enacted in the 1980s, international architectural design has flowed across China's vast land, along with foreign investments, technologies, management techniques, and lifestyles. Grand theaters have had the most profound impact on Chinese cities so far.[34] The Shanghai Grand Theater set the first example of introducing international design in a cultural megastructure. After its completion in 1998, other cities followed suit. Our database includes details of 108 grand theaters, each of which consists of two or three performance halls. Of these grand theaters, forty-eight are designed by foreign architects. These forty-eight theaters are mostly located in the first-tier and "new first-tier" cities like Shanghai, Beijing, Shenzhen, Guangzhou, Chongqing, and Nanjing. In Shanghai, eight out of nine theaters are designed by foreign architects. In terms of the architecture firms that designed the most theaters, gmp holds first place (Figure 7), with six works, followed by Carlos Ott with five; Paul Andreu and Arata Isozaki designed four theaters (or concert halls) each and both Zaha Hadid and Jean-Marie Charpentier designed three theaters (Table 2). The Chinese architectural circle made up their minds to learn from the West and started to follow international trends in the 1980s. Even after forty years of chasing international trends, Chinese architects have yet to radiate their influence beyond China. Even in the competitions for important cultural megastructures, Chinese architects are usually only design partners to the international architects, mostly translating the foreign design into a buildable document. From the client's point of view, an international architect's signature may add value to the built product and satisfy their ambition to reach "international standards." Wherever the design comes from, the client just hopes to have proper work for their performance and branding purposes.

5. Conclusion: The Quest for the Public

This article has briefly summarized the development of grand theater buildings as part of the wave of construction that has flourished in Chinese cities in the 21st century. The construction of grand theaters is motivated by the demand for economic development, high-cultural events, competition between cities, and the ambition to enhance the city's image. After more than 400 grand theaters have entered operation, first-, second-, and third-tier cities are adequately equipped with this type of cultural megastructure. In terms of seats per thousand people, Chinese cities may be in the world's front rankings. However, the new, glamorous theaters are primarily concentrated in the coastal cities and are built in the new districts and new towns, far from the dense, old cities where most residents are concentrated. Many grand theaters are the decorative elements of a new town, central business district, or cultural district. They stand proudly in front of water or on a velvet lawn, shutting out the ordinary "man on the street." The majority of taxpayers and grassroots people have no chance of sharing in the noble fruits of the muses and so grand theaters have become more products of festive vanity than everyday places.

The sharp increase in the number of grand theaters has created a huge market for cultural building design. They add glorious pages to international star architects' shining portfolios. However, Chinese architects have not yet obtained sufficient opportunities to design these artistic mansions. Only a couple of Chinese design firms have managed to break the monopoly of foreign designers, like MAD, Xiang Bingren, Zhang Jinqiu, Cheng Taining, and ECADI. To clear the path, management and municipal committees should give more opportunities to local architects.

Hundreds of grand theaters crystalized the hope, wisdom, prosperity, and expectations of Chinese cities and people at the beginning of the 21st century. We humbly hope that these cultural megastructures can really improve people's lives and lead to the healthy development of cities.

Acknowledgments

The authors heartily thank Dr. Wang Ying for suggestions and comments.

Notes

1. Fumihiko Maki, *Investigations in Collective Form* (St. Louis: Washington University, School of Architecture, 1964).
2. Reyner Banham, *Megastructure: Urban Futures of the Recent Past* (New York: Harper & Row Publishers, 1976).
3. Kenneth Frampton, *Megaform as Urban Landscape*, ed. Brian Carter (United States: University of Michigan, A. Alfred Taubman College of Architecture + Urban Planning, 1999).
4. Jianzhu Shouzhang C., *Giant Utopias and Prefabricated Buildings*, https://mp.weixin.qq.com/s/RLU9-qwQo-aDFwI5eJ-vHQ. The definition of cultural megastructure comes from, in part, as described by Sun Cong in *The Production of Cultural Mega-structures and Making of Chinese City Centers – Taking Grand Theaters as Example*, City University of Hong Kong, PhD thesis draft, 2021.
5. Peter Murray, *The Saga of the Sydney Opera House: The Dramatic Story of the Design and Construction of the Icon of Modern Australia* (New York and London: Spon Press, 2004).
6. Michael J. Grenfell, *Pierre Bourdieu: Agent Provocateur* (London: Continuum, 2004).
7. Theresa Enright, *The Making of Grand Paris* (Cambridge: MIT Press, 2016).
8. Charles Jencks, *The Architecture of the Jumping Universe: A Polemic: How Complexity Science is Changing Architecture and Culture* (London: Academy Editions, 2004).
9. T. C. Chang, "Renaissance Revisited: Singapore as a 'Global City for the Arts'," *International Journal of Urban and Regional Research* 24, no. 4 (2000): 818–831.
10. Lily Kong, Chia-ho Ching, Tsu-lung Chou, Arts, *Culture and the Making of Global Cities – Creating New Urban Landscape in Asia* (Cheltenham: Edward Elgar, 2015); Anna Klingmann, *Brandscapes: Architecture in the Experience Economy* (MIT Press, 2007); John Rennie-Short, Global Metropolitan: *Globalizing Cities in a Capitalist World* (London and New York: Routledge, 2004); London City Hall, *World Cities Cultural Report 2015* (London City Hall, 2016).
11. Ananya Roy and Aihwa Ong, eds., *Worlding Cities: Asian Experiments and the Art of Being Global* (Massachusetts, USA: Wiley-Blackwell, 2011).
12. *Selected Works of Mao Zedong* (Beijing: People's Press, 1991).
13. Pierre Bourdieu, *Distinction: A Social Critique of the Judgement of Taste* (Cambridge: Harvard University Press, 1984).
14. Ministry of Culture, *Wenhua shiye fazhan jiuwu jihua he 2010 nian yuanjing mubiao gangyao*, 2007 (Development Plan of Cultural Affairs and the Vision of 2010) (Beijing: Ministry of Culture, 2007).
15. Sharon Zukin, *Landscape of Power: From Detroit to Disney World* (Berkeley: University of California Press, 1993).
16. 人民网 财经 (Financial Sector of *People's Daily* online), 2021/1/25, http://finance.people.com.cn/BIG5/n1/2021/0125/c1004-32010186.html.
17. About the theater and performances in London, see BBC's report: "There's No Business Like Show Business," The Bottom Line, BBC Radio 4, July 29, 2017 broadcast, http://www.bbc.co.uk/programmes/b08yqb9r, July 29, 2017.
18. The data of Henan Art Center is from author Zhang Lujia's investigation and interview in Zhengzhou, 2017–2021.
19. Ministry of Culture and Tourism of the PRC, *Report on the Investigation of the Development of National Professional Theaters, 2015*, http://www.capa.com.cn/news/showDetail?id=73394, accessed March 20, 2017.
The number of theaters in China in 2018 totaled 1,163: "Theatre Annual Report: Professional theatre performances grew steadily, and the overall utilization rate of venues remained low," Daolue Yanyi, https://mp.weixin.qq.com/s/WNmBb3×iAhCDsWiSV7dQKg
20. Fulong Wu, ed., *Globalization and the Chinese City* (London and New York: Routledge, 2006).
21. Rennie-Short, *Global Metropolitan*.
22. Anne-Marie Broudehoux, *The Making and Selling of Post-Mao Beijing* (New York: Routledge, 2004).
23. "Connecting to the International Track" is a Chinese saying that means to "be in line with the international practice." Before China joined the World Trade Organization (WTO) in 2001, every trade of business was concerned with and hoped to be in line with the international norm.
24. Charlie Xue, *World Architecture in China* (Hong Kong: Joint Publishing Co. Ltd., 2010).
25. Charles Landry, *The Creative City: A Toolkit for Urban Renovators* (London: Earthscan, 2008).
26. Greater London Authority, *London Cultural Capital: Mayor's Cultural Strategies February 2003* (London, England: Greater London Authority).
27. London City Hall, *World Cities Cultural Report 2015*.
28. *Henan Yishu zhongxin jianyi shu* (Proposal of building Henan Art Center), Henan Government, 2004.
29. The nicknames of the theaters developed mostly from the designers' "story-telling" tactics employed when bidding for the project; from there, these nicknames became extensively adopted by the management, mass media, and the public.
30. Roy and Ong, *Worlding Cities*.
31. ibid.
32. From "*Zhongguo chengshi wenhua jingzhengli yanjiu baogao*" (Report of Cultural Competitiveness of Chinese Cities, 2016), Research Institute of Cultural Development, Communication University of China, August 2017.
33. This public crowding situation was learnt of from an interview on July 3, 2017 with the general manager of Shanghai Grand Theater, Ms. Zhang Xiaoding, and engineer Wu Zhihua, and executive officer Pan Lan, Shanghai Grand Theater.
34. Charlie Xue, *World Architecture in China* and Charlie Xue, ed., *Grand Theater Urbanism: Chinese Cities in the 21st Century* (Singapore: Springer, 2019).

Figure Credits

Figure 1: People's Auditorium: (left) Chongqing, 1954; (right) Wuhan, 1959 (authors' photos).
Figure 2: Concert Hall, Shanghai Symphony Orchestra, Shanghai, 2013; designed by Arata Isozaki and Tongji Architectural Design (Group) Co., Ltd. (authors' photos).
Figure 3: Henan Art Center, 2009; designed by PPA Architects, in collaboration with AVIC's design institute (authors' photo).
Figure 4: Jiangsu Grand Theater, 2019 (author's photo).
Figure 5: The symbolizations of a grand theater:
Beijing National theater (photo courtesy of Fu Xing); Oriental Art Center of Shanghai (authors' photo); Fuzhou Strait Culture and Art Center (photo courtesy of PES Architects); and Wuxi Grand Theater (photo courtesy of PES Architects).
Figure 6: (Left) Taichung Opera House; (right) Performing Art Center in Kaohsiung. Both theaters provide ample interior space for public activities (authors' photos).
Figure 7: Two grand theaters designed by gmp: (left) Chongqing Grand Theater, 2009 (authors' photos); (right) Qingdao Grand Theater, 2011 (photo courtesy of gmp © Christian Gahl).

Challenges in Authentic Participatory Mechanisms and Processes: A Case of Involuntary Resettlement in Mumbai, India

Shantanu KHANDKAR, Independent Researcher

Abstract

Any public project that results in the involuntary resettlement of affected communities must incorporate an element of public participation. However, authentic participation is often precluded by considerations that put the project's aims above the interests of the affected communities. This paper investigates such a case of involuntary resettlement caused by the Mumbai Urban Transport Project. The study looks at the role of non-governmental organizations (NGOs), community-based organizations (CBOs), and government bodies, as well as their relationships with the affected communities. The case reveals how participation can be used as a way to legitimize involuntary resettlement; it also illustrates the problems that can be caused by a lack of authentic participation. This paper attempts to illustrate how the state exercises its decision-making powers while simultaneously retreating from any responsibility to include the affected populations in the decision-making process, using token participation as a way of giving a veneer of legitimacy to the entire process.

Author Information
Shantanu KHANDKAR: shantanu.khandkar@gmail.com

Keywords

Resettlement, participation, urban poor, housing, NGOs.

Figure 1
View of resettlement buildings in Lallubhai Compound showing the lack of space between buildings, Mankhurd

1. Introduction

The impacts of displacement as a result of infrastructure development have been extensively discussed in research literature. Sociologists have insisted that although infrastructure investment does massively benefit society, those displaced by such projects bear a disproportionate share of their costs. The World Bank Operational Manual (OP) 4.12 acknowledges the consequences endured by the affected populations of unmitigated involuntary resettlement caused by development projects: reduced incomes, loss of employment, homelessness, and disruptions of social networks. The World Bank's position has been to minimize the various impacts of resettlement on affected populations by providing safeguards that protect their interests.

The term "involuntary resettlement" in itself is a problematic one, as "involuntary" signifies that the affected population has no control over the situation and has not been able to give informed consent; however, "resettlement" implies that the displaced population has been sufficiently compensated for the hardship caused by their displacement. This exposes an inherent power imbalance, where the prerogative of deciding what "resettlement" means does not lie with those who are being resettled. The only way to address this power imbalance is for members of the affected population to be allowed the right to be involved in meaningful consultations and thus, to become participants in their own resettlement, as stakeholders in the project for which they are being displaced, allowing them to improve their lives after they are resettled. This is where authentic participation becomes of paramount importance as an indispensable component of involuntary resettlement. In the absence of authentic participation, the participatory process can become, at worst, an attempt at legitimizing involuntary resettlement without actually overcoming its inherent injustices.

This paper examines the World Bank–funded Mumbai Urban Transport Project (MUTP) through the lens of the intersection of the two intrinsically linked issues of involuntary resettlement and authentic participation. The Mumbai Urban Transport Project Resettlement and Rehabilitation (R&R) Policy (R&R policy) was devised with the objective of minimizing the hardships caused to affected people and improving their living conditions by implementing community participation in the resettlement process. The MUTP R&R policy was formulated to adhere to (Operational Directives) OD 4.30 of the World Bank Involuntary Resettlement policy.

A study carried out by a team of doctors, architects, and planners in two of the resettlement colonies in April 2018 showed a higher prevalence of tuberculosis among the residents of those colonies than in the general population. The two colonies—Lallubhai Compound and Natwar Parekh Compound—are located in the M-East municipal ward on the northeastern fringe of Mumbai. The results showed a direct correlation between the incidence of tuberculosis and the design of the buildings. The lack of natural light and ventilation, and the unhygienic conditions in the colonies were the major factors exacerbating the existing poor environmental conditions in the localities where the colonies were situated.[1]

The deplorable conditions in the resettlement colonies were found to be the result of a relaxation of the building norms that would normally apply to buildings with such high densities (Figure 1). These relaxations were part of the government's prevailing slum policies, and the provisions of the R&R policy were derived from these slum policies. Lallubhai Compound and the Natwar Parekh Compound, although not necessarily representative of all resettlement colonies, serve to highlight several lacunae in the R&R policy.

This paper is structured into four parts as follows: the first part sets up the theoretical premise of the argument by examining the concept of participation through a review of the literature on the concept of participatory planning in general and on participatory mechanisms and actors in Mumbai in particular. The second part looks at the prevailing policies and follows the timeline of the MUTP R&R project to understand the chain of events that affected the participatory mechanisms employed, drawing on government archives, reports from the World Bank, the Tata Institute of Social Sciences (TISS), and the Mumbai Metropolitan Region Development Authority (MMRDA), as well as accounts from the various stakeholders involved in the process. The third part is an analysis of the participatory mechanisms and the fourth part sets out the study's main findings and conclusions.

2. Theoretical Premise

Despite the fact that development projects are supposedly undertaken in the public's interest, the "public" in this context is often conceived as a group that excludes the city's poorer sections, mainly prioritizing middle-class interests.[2] This exclusion results in the displacement of the poor in the pursuit of hegemonic principles that are imposed as what Nancy Fraser, philosopher and critical theorist, calls "the common sense of the day," establishing "the existing order as natural and/or just."[3] Fraser goes on to say that the circulation of such normative discourses is then used to produce consent in the public sphere, which includes just enough participation and representation of multiple interests and perspectives to allow most people to identify with it most of the time. Fraser argues that it would be preferable instead, to recognize a multiplicity of competing publics. Authentic participation could then be understood as an avenue through which the public sphere can be populated—not a single, exclusive, and dominant public—but by multiple publics in deliberation.

Planning is often a struggle between competing aspirations for a shared resource such as space. In this struggle, there are typically those whose aspirations are recognized and catered to and those whose aspirations are marginalized.

This marginalized group has been described in various ways. Arjun Appadurai, anthropologist and globalization theorist, called them "citizens without a city."[4] Sandeep Pendse, in his 1995 essay *Toil, Sweat and the City* coined the term "toilers" and described them as a non-homogenous, divided, and undefined mass, constantly in flux and full of contradictions and ambiguities that defy any attempt at precise delineation.

These "toilers," Pendse wrote, are "relegated to the periphery of existence in the city, both literally and figuratively, actually and ideologically ... the effort, not always successful, is to shift [them] to outlying sectors at a distance from the nerve centers and the arterial routes and, if possible, from each other. Rational space utilization, efficient urban planning, smoother civic operations, uninterrupted traffic flows, and even aesthetic considerations are advanced as goals. All these may be genuinely considered valid by the formulators of the plans."[5]

Pendse further observed that by relegating this section of society to the literal and figurative margins of the city, their lives and realities are kept hidden. In the imagination of the elite and middle classes, the toilers become "unnecessary invaders of the city, burdens that endanger the city, creators of problems that need to be controlled and managed."[6] The deprivation of the right to have their aspirations and interests inform the decisions that affect them becomes, in this case, the defining characteristic of the community.

In light of the above, we shall now discuss a few relevant examples from the abundance of literature discussing public or community participation. Sherry Arnstein's ladder of participation is a useful tool for analyzing the depth of participation—that is, the level of influence the community has on the formulation and implementation of policies.[7] Marissa Choguill built on this idea to develop a ladder for developing countries.[8] King et al. differentiated between unauthentic and authentic participation and contended that authentic participation goes beyond finding the right tools and techniques, as it involves rethinking the roles of, and relationships, between administrators and citizens.[9] Frances Cleaver, in a journal article, mentioned the need for increased government responsiveness and support to help citizens sustain their efforts.[10]

In India, much of this discourse is focused on the roles of NGOs (non-governmental organizations) and CBOs (community-based organizations). These rose to prominence in the years following the liberalization of the economy in the early 1990s, when the policy environment took a turn toward neoliberalism. In the case of housing policies, central government control was deemphasized in favor of local governments, NGOs, and the market. These changes were partly intended to democratize development through the involvement of local agencies and communities, making the active participation of communities more important than ever. Because local knowledge is instrumental in the success of development strategies, the need for participation led to a proliferation of CBOs and NGOs; these organizations act as a means for civil society to assert itself. In a process that Appadurai called "deep democracy," these groups join together to mobilize community organizations to step into the vacuum created by a withdrawing state, to mediate the interests of the urban poor.[11] John F. C. Turner identified three roles for NGOs—as enablers of CBOs, mediators between communities and agencies, and advisors and as consultants to authorities.[12]

However, NGOs have attracted criticism on the grounds that their very existence accelerates the withdrawal of the state, a process David Harvey described as "privatization by NGO."[13] NGOs have been described as the "Trojan horses of global neoliberalism."[14] It should be noted that, notwithstanding their own sincerity and commitment to promoting the interests of their clientele, NGOs, by their nature, lack any comprehensive accountability to the populace as a whole.

Another important aspect of community participation pertains to the interests that inform the decisions and the agencies that formulate the information systems. It can be argued that information systems are almost never neutral and are often influenced by powerful people outside the context of intervention, and that they can become "a playground for their interests."[15] Authentic participation, therefore, is precluded by information systems that are not equipped to conceptualize the highly complex sets of relationships that exist on the ground.

It is, thus, necessary to examine whether the participatory mechanisms devised for MUTP were capable of providing authentic participation and whether the interests of the PAP (project-affected people) were given primacy.

3. Effects of the Neoliberal Policy Environment in Mumbai on Resettlement Policies

As per the R&R policy, the overwhelming majority of the project-affected households (PAHs) that fell into the "squatter" category were entitled to a tenement of 20.91 square meters under the provisions of the slum redevelopment policy. The currently prevailing Slum Redevelopment Scheme came into being in 1995 through an amendment of the Maharashtra Slum Areas (Improvement, Clearance, and Redevelopment) Act, 1971. It was representative of the general shift in the policy environment toward neoliberal principles at that time. Some of the salient features of the policy are the use of market forces for cost recovery, with the introduction of incentives for developers and in-situ resettlement and clear tenure for slum dwellers; the government plays an enabling role.[16]

Under the new model, a quasi-government body known as the Slum Redevelopment Authority (SRA) was established as a single agency to oversee the redevelopment projects; slum dwellers could form cooperative societies and register them with the SRA. Registered societies could then get a developer to submit a redevelopment proposal for SRA approval. The quid pro quo was that the slum dwellers would be entitled to a 23.21-square-meter house free of cost, while the developer would receive an incentive in terms of Floor Space Index (FSI) to build market-rate housing on the same site. Any incentive in FSI that could not be consumed on-site would be given as Transferable Development Rights (TDRs) for use elsewhere.[17]

One can identify several problems with this policy. First, many redevelopment schemes for slums in locations that were deemed undesirable for sale on the open market failed to take off. Second, the apartments provided for resettlement purposes often did not suit the slum dwellers' work patterns; they found it more profitable to sell them off to lower- and middle-income group buyers who found them more attractive.[18] Third, because the rehabilitation component of the project was subsidized by the sale component, the cost of the saleable apartments increased, making them even more unaffordable.

However, an important aspect of the criticism of the SRA's approach is that it served the interests of the developers more than those of the slum dwellers. The additional development rights awarded as incentives made the already dense slum areas even denser, without an infrastructure capable of sustaining this. To accommodate the density, building norms relating to the dimensions of various rooms, open spaces, and the spacing between buildings were relaxed, leading to the deterioration of environmental conditions.

The policy called for provisions for "obligatory participation" from landowners and occupants of the slum areas.[19] This was in contrast to the past, when there were little to no explicit requirements for public participation in the formulation of policies.

It should be noted that the slum policies emanate from the state governments. There is no specific central government policy with regard to slums—meaning, slums on central government land have a situation distinct from those located on state government or municipal government land.

4. The Mumbai Urban Transport Project and Resettlement of the Affected Population

The Mumbai Urban Transport Project was conceived in 1994, with the objective of updating the transportation infrastructure in the Mumbai Metropolitan Region (MMR), which had failed to keep up with traffic growth. The project had a rail-based component and a road-based component. It required the acquisition of 59.02 hectares of land and the resettlement of 19,228 households (which later grew to about 23,000), which was an unprecedented scale of resettlement. The R&R of the PAP formed the third component of the MUTP.

According to data available from baseline surveys in 2002, 99.4 percent of the 19,228 households identified for resettlement were squatters with no tenurial rights to the land they were occupying. A total of 40 percent of the households fell below the poverty line, with an income of less than INR 2,500 per month. On average, the monthly familial income was INR 2,978 (a little above US$61 at the 2002 exchange rate). As many as 91 percent of the houses were below 20 square meters in area and less than 1 percent had toilets and individual taps for water supply.[20]

So that the MUTP could become eligible for World Bank funding, it adopted a comprehensive R&R policy in March 1997, conforming to the guidelines of OD 4.30. This policy, which was later updated in December 2000, laid down the guidelines for the resettlement options and entitlements of the PAP.

The R&R policy explicitly stated that the resettlement would be carried out with community participation and to that extent, NGOs and CBOs were tasked with devising and implementing participatory processes. In addition to the involvement of NGOs and CBOs to ensure community participation, the policy also called for the involvement of the private sector to offset the costs of construction related to resettlement. Private developers who would provide buildings free of cost for resettlement would be reimbursed with various incentives. The involvement of both the private sector and NGOs was highlighted as an "innovative approach."[21]

5. The Case of the Railway Slums and the Role of NGOs

In actuality, efforts to foster community participation in creating resilient communities in slums had preceded the MUTP by a few decades. NGOs and CBOs had already been active in some slum communities, working to ameliorate the living conditions in those areas. The success of these efforts was what led to the appointment of these NGOs and CBOs as representatives of civil society in the MUTP R&R project.

Mumbai's slums are located on land belonging to private landowners, as well as the government. Vast tracts of land in Mumbai are owned by central, state, and local government agencies, as well as parastatal bodies such as the Airport Authority of India, Mumbai Port Trust, and Indian Railways, which are public undertakings of the government of India that answer directly to their headquarters, while operating within the geographical boundaries of local government bodies.

When the MUTP was conceptualized, there were about 25,000 families in Mumbai living in shanties built barely a meter away from the suburban railway tracks (Figure 2). This was an extremely dangerous and stressful living situation that also adversely affected the efficiency and productivity of the trains, which had to move slowly when traveling through the slums.

Because the slums were on land owned by Indian Railways (IR), the provisions of the state slum policy did not apply to them. The state, regardless of its policy, could not provide the slum dwellers with basic amenities like water, sanitation, or electricity. IR would not allow any such work, as it would be

Figure 2
Slum adjoining railway tracks near Bandra station, Bandra

seen as a tacit legitimization of the encroachment. Other slums existing on land belonging to central government bodies also faced the same issue. Thus, the conditions in these slums were much worse than those on state government and municipal lands.[22]

A group of three NGOs had been working with the railway slum dwellers to try to improve their living conditions and protect them against demolition without resettlement. The Alliance, as it was called, was formed by the Society for Promotion of Area Resource Centers (SPARC), the National Slum Dwellers' Federation (NSDF), and Mahila Milan (MM).

SPARC was founded in 1984 by professionals who had previous experience working with more traditional welfare-based NGOs. Their work was concerned with training women's groups from pavement-dwelling families to survey their settlements and use the data collected to campaign for secure tenure. MM, a women's savings and credit group, grew out of SPARC's work with the women. NSDF was a community-based organization formed by associations of slum dwellers joining together to organize the poor to fight demolitions and secure basic amenities.[23]

In 1988, SPARC worked with the government to undertake a census of the slums along the railway tracks. The enumeration led to the formation of the railway slum dwellers' own collective, the Railway Slum Dwellers Federation (RSDF). The RSDF opened negotiations with the government regarding the slum dwellers' willingness to move, provided they were given secure tenure after resettlement. They even identified five plots nearby where resettlement could take place.

When the need arose to relocate a settlement of 900 families to build a new railway link, the community was ready. Most of the families were offered government-built houses a short distance away from their original locations for INR 58,000 each. About 150 families who could not afford this price identified a plot adjacent to the government housing and proposed that they be allowed to build their own houses. The state provided the land and infrastructure, while The Alliance supported the design, construction, and financing of the houses. The new houses cost about one-third of the government-built houses. The strong relationship between the state government, Indian Railways, and SPARC led to a peaceful transition of the families who moved voluntarily into transit housing. This exercise created a protocol for managing later relocations. The experiment was carried further when SPARC worked with Indian Railways to successfully persuade the families living closest to the tracks to move about 9 meters away and for a wall to be built to prevent further encroachments. As a confidence-building exercise, SPARC even raised funds to build a wall adjacent to one settlement.[24]

The Alliance devised a methodology that would involve the community and develop the local capacity for data collection, ensuring that the community would be motivated and empowered to be involved in their own relocation. Initially, the "chalk mark" method was used, where the NSDF leader and residents would mark the doors on the houses with a piece of chalk. This was supposed to trigger the process of participation as inhabitants would inevitably start asking questions about why their doors were being marked. The opportunity could then be taken to explain the details of the project and the residents could then get involved by making their own suggestions about how the houses should be numbered and what criteria should be applied for enumeration. This was followed by a rough mapping and numbering. Once the numbering was done, a cadastral-type survey was conducted, and a settlement profile was prepared. Where they were willing, the households were grouped into units of fifty, and another round of data checking was carried out. The communities were also encouraged to take family photographs and create identity cards for themselves.[25]

The repeated interaction allowed a rapport to develop between The Alliance and the community. Whenever individuals who felt threatened by the survey or who wanted to obstruct it stepped forward, the surveyors would leave, making no attempt to tackle or diffuse the situation. For this reason, the surveyors were accompanied by NSDF and/or SPARC workers from the area.

6. The Beginning of Community Participation Under the MUTP

Based on this relationship and their success in implementing community participation and cooperation in the railway slums, the NGOs were asked to become part of a task force appointed to formulate a comprehensive R&R Policy for the MUTP. The involvement of NGOs as proponents of civil society became part of the policy and not an arbitrary government decision.

The process of formulating a policy in accordance with World Bank guidelines for the R&R component of the MUTP began in 1995. For this purpose, the group of ministers (GoM) appointed a task force composed of government officials, representatives of the project implementation agencies, practicing lawyers, architects, and housing-finance institutions. Civil society was represented on the task force by SPARC and NSDF. This task force also identified possible relocation sites. The R&R policy was adopted in March 1997 and further amended in December 2000.

The next step consisted of carrying out Baseline Socio-Economic Surveys (BSES). The findings of the BSES were to guide the further progress of the program. The BSES was considered the first stage of community participation; the community-approved database that was produced at this stage would effectively delineate the scope of the resettlement and the entitlements of the various groups of PAP. The eligibility of PAP for resettlement was based on their being enumerated during the BSES.

In April 2002, the MMRDA released a Resettlement Action Plan (RAP). The RAP was drawn up with the involvement of the NGOs and consisted of the policy and institutional framework for the R&R project.

Pursuant to the requirements laid down in OD 4.30, the MUTP R&R policy stated that the Draft RAP should include provisions for "community participation and integration with host populations."[26] Accordingly, the RAP laid down the main techniques used to ensure public participation. The responsibility for ensuring community participation was placed upon the NGOs. Apart from conducting BSES, the NGOs were also involved in the implementation of the R&R by being involved in the preparation of Resettlement Implementation Plans (RIPs) and Community Environment Management Plans (CEMPs) for individual sites. The NGOs conducted meetings for the PAP to work out the various components of the RIPs, such as updating the BSES, when required, and selecting resettlement sites. In these meetings, an attempt was made to develop the design of the dwelling units. However, the small size of the apartments and the budgetary constraints left little room for innovation; in other cases, the communities were prepared to accept available dwelling units. The NGOs were given responsibility for a wide range of activities before, during, and after the resettlement.

To procure dwelling units, land tenure, and land transfer, the RAP provided for the use of the TDR policy. According to the policy, if landowners or developers agreed to build resettlement units of 20.91 square meters each and hand them over to the government free of cost, they would be entitled to development rights equivalent to the FSI on the land surrendered and the FSI consumed in the construction of the houses.[27]

Sites were identified around the city for acquisition, from government bodies as well as private landowners. It should be noted that the sites obtained from private landowners were either under non-buildable reservations or on the outskirts of the city.[28]

7. Findings

As mentioned before, the NGOs' work with the railway slums had created a strong working relationship between the various actors, leading to an effective process of participation. However, the same was not necessarily true in the case of the road-based component of the MUTP. Sources indicate that the relationship between the parties—that is, the NGOs, the government, and the PAP—broke down. A review of the correspondence between the parties and the reports by the bodies involved shows that there were three main reasons for this breakdown, namely: 1. the differences in the context of the PAP in the road and rail-based components; 2. a lack of capacity on the part of the NGOs; and 3. mistrust between the parties.

Some PAP who were unhappy with their relocation wrote to the Inspection Committee of the World Bank asking them to intervene. The Inspection Panel reported receiving up to four distinct requests from associations of shopkeepers and residents affected by the road component.

The grievances of the PAP and the initial difficulties faced by relocated households were capitalized on by politicians and presented as failures. When this happened, the government assigned blame to the NGOs for failing in project implementation.

A discussion of the grievances put forward by these "requesters," the management response, the Inspection Panel's report, and the Impact Assessment Report presented to the World Bank by TISS in March 2008 help highlight some pertinent themes in the nature of the participatory process of the project.

7.1 The Differences in the Contexts

The Inspection Panel's report points out that there were major differences in the demographics between the PAP in the case of the railway slums and those in the road component. The railway slums consisted mostly of socially and economically weaker sections. Living next to the railway tracks in temporary housing with no access to basic infrastructure, their living conditions were far worse than the road component PAP. For them, resettlement represented a chance at a better life. The same could not be said for the road component PAP. This group included several middle-income shopkeepers who also generated employment for others. Their needs for space and income restoration were different. The resettlement program was largely based on the provisions of the SRA in terms of entitlements and failed to identify the heterogeneity of the PAP and their needs. In the case of Lallubhai Compound, 84.6 percent of shopkeepers reported a decrease in clientele post-relocation and 76.9 percent reported a decrease in overall viability. A total of 42.3 percent of shop owners were unable to afford to keep on their previous employees.[29]

7.2 Lack of Capacity on the Part of NGOs

There were several points of conflict between SPARC, MMRDA, and the World Bank. While the World Bank, quite understandably, pushed for all procedures to be centralized and standardized as per international standards, the procedures devised by the NGOs stemmed from their experience in working with the communities and their desire to foster community participation. These procedures were more inclined toward mobilizing the community and allowing the local actors to learn and grow with the process. The inaccuracies and gaps in data—which admittedly were the products of the nature of the documentation itself—would be corrected over time.

The NGOs had decided to use the people from the communities to conduct the surveys. However, the staff carrying out the surveys were not given sufficient training on the type of information required and its links with the project characteristics. For example, some NGOs stated that their staff received about two mornings of training before the survey started.[30] There was little to no supervision on the part of the MMRDA, which stemmed from their own lack of capacity. The method of surveying left many key decisions to the subjective discretion of the surveyors. The procedure has been characterized as "some form of self-reporting improvised by the affected groups themselves."[31] The merits of this are open to debate, but there were tangible problems, such as the failure on the part of the NGO staff to record houses' upper stories. There was no consensus among individual surveyors on what was to be reported, who was to be counted, what the definitions of a "family" or a "household" were, or what constituted an identifiable "structure" which, given the nature of the built form in the affected areas, could be a subjective matter. This resulted in inaccuracies in data that negatively affected the planning for the project and the outlook of the PAP toward the NGOs and the government.

7.3 Mistrust Between the Parties

Some PAP complained that the NGOs and the MMRDA did not allow them access to the survey sheets to verify the results. According to some, there was confusion at the time of the surveys regarding their actual purpose. Many later told the Inspection Panel that at the time of the survey, they had not even heard of the MUTP.[32]

Some PAP claimed that their "rights to participation and consultation were effectively denied" and that their "attempts to raise [their] concerns were not successful."[33] The management response to these claims was that the MMRDA had held several meetings with the PAP and that SPARC was in a continuous consultation process with the PAP. Several of the PAP described the consultation meetings as being like a "fish market" on account of their chaotic nature.[34] The informal nature of some of these consultations meant that what actually transpired at these meetings remains a matter of contention. According to the Inspection Panel, any consensus arrived at would more than likely have been partial and based on many PAP not being able to make themselves heard in the public meetings. The authenticity of the minutes of the meetings held by the MMRDA and elected representatives with the PAP was challenged by several PAP in letters to the World Bank.

The letters written by several organizations of PAP to the World Bank Inspection Panel indicate an extremely acrimonious relationship between them and the NGOs. The letters accuse SPARC of corrupt practices, bullying, and denying them the resettlements to which they were entitled unless their demands were met. This allegation is alluded to in the Impact Assessment (IA) report prepared by TISS in 2008. The IA report says that the PAP's entitlement to receive a "pucca house"[35] with clear tenure created many vested interests. Many middlemen/brokers emerged, promising to help slum dwellers who were not PAP acquire a house or a shop under the scheme; some PAP were also lured into selling or renting out their structures. Such practices were encouraged due to the intervention of locally influential persons such as slumlords and local politicians. The report also alleges that certain PAP themselves resorted to dubious means like overnight partitioning of their structures into a house or a shop to claim double entitlements, or presenting forged documents to obtain benefits. A survey conducted in three resettlement sites after a few years of resettlement showed that more than 15 percent of the resettlement houses had been rented out or sold to outsiders for various reasons.[36] The report noted that it was conceivable in such a situation that the names of certain NGO or MMRDA staff members could be used to give legitimacy to the claims of such middlemen. Also, according to the report, one of the NGOs (which remains unnamed in the report) expressed concern that their public image was being actively maligned by these vested interests. Although it is beyond the scope of this paper to investigate the veracity of any of these allegations, their existence does, however, show the mutual mistrust—warranted or otherwise—that existed between the PAP, the NGOs, and the government authorities.

8. Conclusion

The nature of community participation in the MUTP R&R project can be analyzed on the basis of two main premises. The first is that the policy framework precluded any authentic participation. The second is that the interests addressed in the resettlement were not those of the PAP.

Two aspects of the policy framework are discussed below, namely, the role of the NGOs and the lack of access.

In the case of the MUTP, it is clear that the state placed the entire onus of ensuring community participation on the NGOs and abdicated all responsibility on the same. Although the NGOs made efforts to overcome their own lack of capacity, there is little evidence that there was any active institutional or logistical support extended by the government beyond benign neglect.

The trust and mutual understanding that existed between the railway slum dwellers and NGOs seem to have been absent in their relationship with other PAP. According to the RAP, SPARC had been engaged to ensure community participation based on their previous and ongoing relationship with the railway slum community. The assumption that the same kind of relationship could be fostered in a short time with other PAP failed to take into consideration that the relationship with the railway slum community had grown over more than fifteen years of interaction, or that their history with PAP from the road component of the MUTP was quite different. Also, the capacity of the NGOs to conduct an exercise of a much greater scale and complexity than what had been needed in the railway slums was overestimated. As the Inspection Panel report puts it, "the NGOs involved became in effect two small agencies contractually employed by the government, with insufficient capacity, decreasing status, and declining abilities to act as exponents of civil society."[37]

A crucial factor in any truly participatory process is that the participants need to have free access to information regarding the process and that there is a free exchange of views between the community and the administrators. Only when the community is assured that their views and opinions will not only be heard, but also acted upon, can they be truly invested in the participatory process. Participation at an early stage of project design enables the views of the community to be incorporated in the project design. This, too, seems to have been compromised. The resettlement model left little opportunity for decision making. The participants may have felt betrayed by, and dissatisfied with the outcome of their input during the consultation.

A discussion of the participatory framework points to a fundamental problem of the motivations for developing the framework. An argument could be made that the state aimed for token participation, at best, to qualify for funding and to deflect responsibility for any failures onto the community. Moreover, these policies led to the PAP's interests not being given primacy.

The use of TDRs in procuring the sites for resettlement may have contributed to restricting the choices of resettlement sites from those most favorable to the PAP, to those more profitable for developers and landowners. The TDR policy created a vested interest for the private sector to purchase and develop land in cheaper locations and use the development rights to build more profitable housing in higher-income areas. Thus, the motivation for choosing resettlement sites may well have been to the benefit of the developers, rather than to the best interests of the PAP.

One of the objectives of the R&R policy was to "develop and execute resettlement plans in such a manner that displaced persons are compensated for their losses at replacement cost prior to the actual move."[38] The absence of economic analysis of the displacement and resettlement operations in the project was noted in a memorandum sent on May 12, 1999, by the World Bank regional vice-president, South Asian region, to the country director, India, which commented that there was no intention of including the resettlement costs along with the building of the rail project to test whether the project would make economic sense,[39] pointing to a less-than-serious approach toward the economic rehabilitation of the PAP.

The case of the MUTP R&R project represents a strange chimera as far as neoliberal development is concerned. Although the government gave the responsibility of delivery to the private sector and that of participation to civil society, the authority to make decisions remained firmly in the hands of the government agencies. Authentic participation implies genuine choice, but there is little to suggest that such a choice, including that of not moving, was ever given to the PAP. On the contrary, they were, for the most part, presented with a *fait accompli* with little input from their side, in contrast to the process that was followed before the MUTP.

As Asian countries follow the infrastructure development paradigm with a rights-based approach to resettlement, it is important to learn from examples such as this that resettlement needs to be seen as an integral part of infrastructure projects and not as an obstacle to be overcome. Furthermore, in the absence of authentic participation—where they are part of the decision-making process and not simply its intended beneficiaries—the affected populations will continue to pay a high price for benefits accrued by others.

Notes

1. Doctors For You, *Studying the Association Between Structural Factors and Tuberculosis in the Resettlement Colonies in M-East Ward, Mumbai* (Mumbai: Mumbai Metropolitan Region-Environment Improvement Society, 2018).
2. Amita Baviskar, "Cows, Cars, and Cycle-rickshaws: Bourgeois Environmentalism and the Battle for Delhi's Streets," in *Elite and Everyman: The Cultural Politics of the Indian Middle Classes*, eds. Amita Baviskar and Raka Ray (Delhi: Routledge India, 2011), 391–418.
3. Nancy Fraser, "Rethinking the Public Sphere: A Contribution to the Critique of Actually Existing Democracy," *Social Text* 25/26 (1990): 22.
4. Arjun Appadurai, "Deep Democracy: Urban Governmentality and the Horizon of Politics," *Environment & Urbanization* 13, no. 2 (October, 2001): 5.
5. Sandeep Pendse, "Toil, Sweat and the City," in *Bombay: Metaphor for Modern India*, eds. Sujata Patel and Alice Thorner (Mumbai: Oxford University Press, 1995), 9.
6. ibid., 10.
7. Sherry R. Arnstein, "A Ladder of Citizen Participation," *Journal of the American Planning Association* 35, no. 4 (1969): 216–24.
8. Marisa B. Choguill, "A Ladder of Community Participation for Underdeveloped Countries," *Habitat International* 20, no. 3 (1996): 431–44.
9. Cheryl S. King, Kathryn M. Feltey, and Bridget O. Susel, "The Question of Participation: Toward Authentic Public Participation in Public Administration," *Public Administration Review* 58, no. 4 (July-August, 1998): 317–27.
10. Frances Cleaver, "Paradoxes of Participation: Questioning Participatory Approaches to Development," *Journal of International Development* 11, no. 4 (July, 1999): 597–612.
11. Appadurai, "Deep Democracy: Urban Governmentality and the Horizon of Politics," 3.
12. John F. C. Turner, *Building Community: A Third World Case Book*, ed. Bertha Turner (London: Community Books, 1988).
13. David Harvey, *A Brief History of Neoliberalism* (Oxford: Oxford University Press, 2005), 177.
14. Tina Wallace, "NGO Dilemmas: Trojan Horses for Global Neoliberalism?" eds. Leo Panitch and Christophe Leys, *Socialist Register* 40 (2003): 1.
15. Prasad Shetty, *Gossip and the City: Investigations into Urban Information Systems* (Rotterdam: Institute for Housing and Urban Development Studies and Erasmus University, 2003), 40.
16. Jan Nijman, "Against the Odds: Slum Rehabilitation in Neoliberal Mumbai," *Cities* 25 (2008): 73–85.
17. Slum Rehabilitation Authority, *Guidelines for the Implementation of Slum Rehabilitation Schemes in Greater Mumbai* (Mumbai: Housing and Special Assistance Department, Government of Maharashtra, 1997).
18. Shetty, *Gossip and the City*, 19.
19. Government of Maharashtra, *Maharashtra Slum Areas (Improvement, Clearance and Redevelopment) Act* (Mumbai: Government Press, 1971), 6.
20. MMRDA, *Mumbai Urban Transport Project Resettlement Action Plan* (Mumbai: MMRDA, 2002), 13–15.
21. World Bank, *Bank Management Response to Request for Inspection Panel Review of the India – Mumbai Urban Transport Project* (Washington D.C.: World Bank, 2004), 6.
22. Sundar Burra, *Resettlement and Rehabilitation of the Urban Poor: the Mumbai Urban Transport Project* (Mumbai: SPARC India, 1999).
23. Sheela Patel, Celine D'Cruz, and Sundar Burra, "Beyond Evictions in a Global City: People-managed Resettlement in Mumbai," *Environment & Urbanization* 14, no. 2 (2002): 159–72.
24. Sheela Patel and Kalpana Sharma, "One David and Three Goliaths: Avoiding Anti-poor solutions to Mumbai's Transport Problems," *Environment & Urbanization* 10, no. 2 (1998): 149–59.
25. Sheela Patel and Sheridan Bartlett, "Reflections on Innovation, Assessment, and Social Change: A SPARC Case Study," *Development in Practice* 19, no. 1 (2009): 3–15.
26. Government of Maharashtra, *Resettlement and Rehabilitation Policy for Mumbai Urban Transport Project* (MUTP) (Mumbai: Government Press, 2000), 9.
27. MMRDA, *Mumbai Urban Transport Project Resettlement Action Plan*, 23–24.
28. MMRDA, *Mumbai Urban Transport Project Resettlement Action Plan*, 39.
29. TISS, *Impact Assessment of Resettlement Implementations under Mumbai Urban Transport Project* (MUTP) (Mumbai: MMRDA, 2008), 86.
30. Inspection Panel, *Investigation Report, India: Mumbai Urban Transport Project* (Washington, D.C.: World Bank, 2005), 64.
31. Inspection Panel, *Investigation Report, India: Mumbai Urban Transport Project*, 67.
32. Inspection Panel, *Investigation Report, India: Mumbai Urban Transport Project*, 66.
33. Inspection Panel, *Investigation Report, India: Mumbai Urban Transport Project*, 99.
34. Ko Takeuchi, *Resettlement as Development? Understanding the Impacts of Resettlement and Rehabilitation in the Mumbai Urban Transport Project*, MA Thesis (Vancouver: University of British Columbia, Faculty of Graduate Studies, Community and Regional Planning, 2007), 69.
35. "Pucca house" (solid house) is a term used in South Asia for houses designed to be stable and permanent. From the Hindi word *pukka* (lit. ripe/cooked). Contrasted with "kutcha house" (lit. raw house) used for temporary and/or flimsily constructed houses.
36. TISS, *Impact Assessment of Resettlement Implementations under Mumbai Urban Transport Project* (MUTP) (Mumbai: MMRDA, 2008), 4.
37. Inspection Panel, *Investigation Report, India: Mumbai Urban Transport Project*, 60.
38. Government of Maharashtra, 2000, *Resettlement and Rehabilitation Policy*, 2.
39. Inspection Panel, *Investigation Report, India: Mumbai Urban Transport Project*, 44.

Figure Credits

Figure 1: View of resettlement buildings in Lallubhai Compound showing the lack of space between buildings, Mankhurd (lecerle, licenced by CC BY-NC—SA 2,0, https://www.Lallubhai flickr.com/photos/lecercle/290249007, February 29, 2008).
Figure 2: Slum adjoining railway tracks near Bandra station, Bandra (w:user:PlaneMad, licensed by CC BY-SA 3.0, via Wikimedia Commons, July 4, 2006).

A Retrospection on "Instafamous Architecture": Historical Framework, Theoretical Relationships, and Evaluation

SUI Yingda, Architectural Designer, Gensler
LIU Yanjie, Architectural Designer, Voice Architecture Lab

Abstract

"Instafamous architecture" is an autonomous architectural movement of the self-media age that has sometimes been alienated and dismissed by the mainstream architectural profession. However, it has never stood alone and is embedded in the history and theory of architecture, and in communication and the economy. This thesis takes a retrospective look at the history of the movement and examines its inevitability through the multidisciplinary theoretical relationships of Instafamous architecture, and it develops a historical and theoretical framework for this missing chapter of modern architectural history. Under this framework, the values and risks of Instafamous architecture are evaluated, drawing the authors to the conclusion that Instafamous architecture reflects the zeitgeist of the contemporary self-media age.

Author Information
SUI Yingda: Yingda.Sui@outlook.com
LIU Yanjie: yj_liu199501@163.com

Keywords

Instafamous architecture, self-media, consumerism, zeitgeist, public interests.

Figure 1
Photo of Taj Mahal in *National Geographic* magazine, March 1921

Prologue: A Missing Chapter of Architectural History

Self-media using mobile internet access has been one of the world's main trends since the 2010s. The new mobile-based online space has become an arena where all the performers—faces, food, products, or scenery—try to capture as much attention as they can from the audience. The winners in this contest are referred to as "Instafamous."

Architecture has not been excluded from this emerging trend. Every day, Instafamous architecture projects are being photographed, published, and marked on self-media worldwide, including Instagram, Facebook, and Weibo. The photo subjects can be urban landmarks, or interior spaces, either designed by renowned architects or artists, or by anonymous sources.

Despite being popular among cybercitizens, such projects are in most cases not highly valued by professionals. Being "Instafamous architecture," these projects are usually excluded from professional discussions—that very aspect used as an excuse to do so. Therefore, although Instafamous architecture is a noticeable enough phenomenon, its historical framework is still missing.

This thesis references Rem Koolhaas's *Delirious New York: A Retrospective Manifesto for Manhattan*[1] in regards to its research methodology. It traces and deduces the origin, incubation, formation, and development of Instafamous architecture, up till the definition and classification were set; the multidisciplinary theoretical relationships of this architectural movement are then discussed. Based on these historical and theoretical frameworks, an evaluation of Instafamous architecture is made. The thesis aims to supply the missing chapter of modern architecture, thus enabling Instafamous architecture to be positioned and accessed.

1. A Brief History of Instafamous Architecture

1.1 Modern Architecture and Mass Media

Modern architecture has always been linked to mass culture. Indeed, in the 20th century, mass media became the true site where architecture was produced, as well as its source of engagement. Architecture historian and theorist Beatriz Colomina suggests that Le Corbusier's "Architectural Promenade" concept was inspired by the way people watch movies. The architectural spaces created by Le Corbusier can be viewed as a continuous set of images: the walls as floating paper and the extended windows as the frame for the scene. The inhabitants receive a movie-like impression as they move freely in the space. Such design also helps the buildings to become icons simply through image-based mass media, exclusive of real experience.[2]

As the film industry further developed, the way architecture associated with media was enhanced by postmodern architects. The movie *Metropolis* by Fritz Lang in 1927 conceived and expressed a surreal future city concept.[3] Fifty years later, Koolhaas used a similar surreal writing style in the script of *Delirious New York* to display the urban history of Manhattan and expressed this as "Manhattanism." At almost the same time, Bernard Tschumi raised "form follows fiction" as an architectural design method, placing spatial narration at the center.

In the modern architectural movements mentioned above, a circular relationship between media and architecture can be traced. Media expresses and deduces architecture simultaneously, regardless of the architects' intent, while the viewers—including the architects—conceive architecture through that media. The conception follows the evolution of media, seeing

Figure 2
An Instagram post on Santorini

Figure 3
An Instagram post on Burano

architecture as images strips or as a narration script. Further, architects may voluntarily participate as motivation for postmodern narrative architecture. This relationship even predicted the arrival of a new architectural movement in the 2010s era of self-media.

1.2 Incubation: Architecture in "Embryonic Self-Media"

Although Twitter, Facebook, and Weibo only came into existence in the 2000s, the mechanism for self-media had actually been in incubation throughout the 20th century. This embryonic self-media predefined the way that people would perceive and propagate architecture in the self-media era.

This long incubation period dates back to the popularization of travel photography. In 1888, a roll-film camera, together with an enlargement service system, was invented by Kodak's founder, George Eastman. These inventions significantly reduced the kit that photographers had to carry while traveling and also separated the photo-developing process from the photographer.[4] After that, the authority to produce images of architecture was no longer monopolized by skilled painters and professional photographers. Instead, the general public, especially travelers, could easily capture and circulate their own perception of architecture as an image. The roll-film camera removed the authority for architectural images from elite architects and local painters, and made it available to the general public.

In the same year that the roll-film camera was invented, *National Geographic* magazine started publishing. Within its pages, architectural photography played an important role (Figure 1). By introducing striking architectural images from around the world to the public, the magazine catered to metropolitan citizens' curiosity about cultures in distant parts of the world.

Figure 4
A collage post on Xiaohongshu highlighting the Xia'men abandoned building

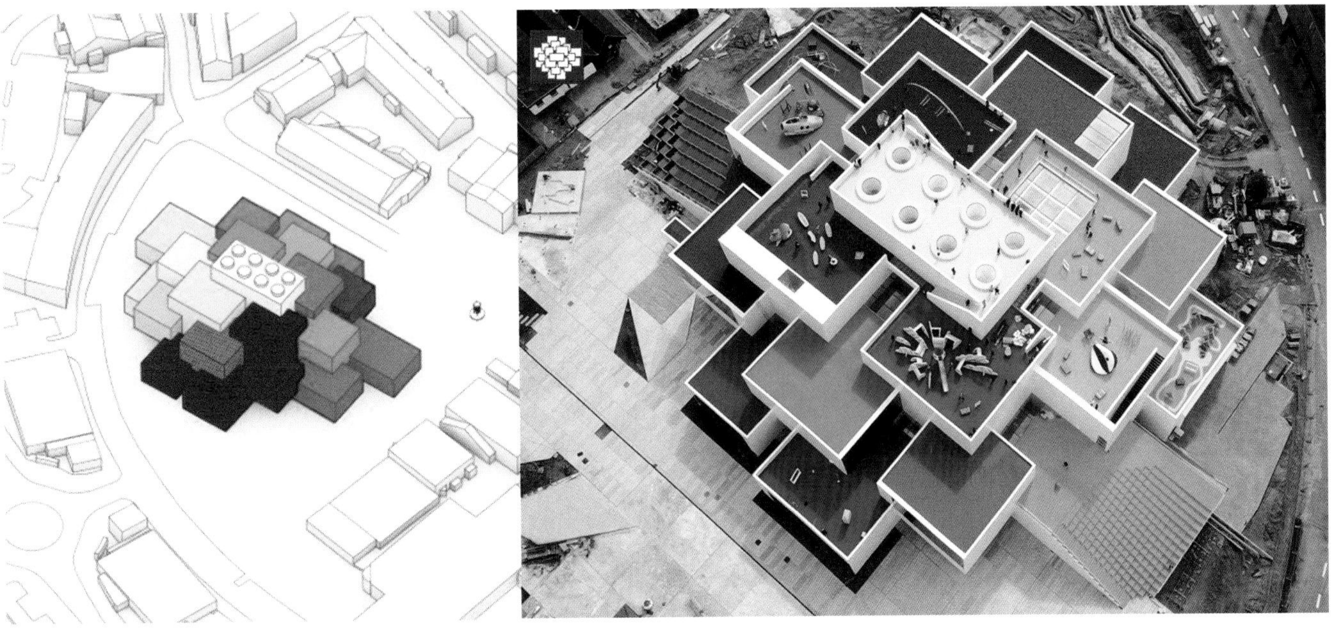

Figure 5
LEGO House by BIG, from diagram to building

Some photographs published by the magazine later became the key images of world architecture in the audience's minds.

In the 1930s, the invention of postcards that used real photographs marked the establishment of the self-media mechanism. By purchasing postcards as souvenirs, penning down a few lines, and sending them to friends and family who had not visited that country or place, tourists voluntarily "shared a post" with them. In the process, architectural photographs that graced these postcards became more well-known, popularizing architecture with distinctive key images, rather than those with a nicer spatial experience.

During this period, architecture seemed to develop a relationship with media through two parallel approaches. In one, architects tried to make architecture a refined and comprehensive art that could be experienced like a film, while in the other, architecture was more and more enjoyed by the public as a popular and simple art of key images.

1.3 Formation: "Wild-Grown" Instafamous Architecture

In 2006, 2009, and 2010, respectively, the self-media platforms of Twitter, Weibo, and Instagram were launched and quickly became important media for architecture. More significantly, the power to propagate or criticize architecture in public, as well as to decide how much an architectural style was propagated, was handed over to netizens.

A post via these mobile applications usually consists of three core elements: photography, geo-tagging, and hashtagging, among which the photograph plays the key role. With this formula, a piece of architecture is summarized and published as follows:

1. With no more than nine representative, attractive images;
2. With a short description—a maximum of 140 characters; sometimes it can be as short as a "nickname;" and
3. With its location.

The mature mechanism of self-media predetermines that architecture with a more pure, but eye-catching image, a more catchy, but understandable nickname, and which are also in Instafamous places, have more chance of gaining popularity. These qualities can be summarized as "Instagrammability," which is an increasingly important life criteria for the younger generation. A survey of 1000 young adults by holiday home insurance company Schofields Insurance Ltd. showed that 40 percent of millennials who grew up with Instagram rated "Instagrammability" as the most important quality of their holiday destination.[5] Not unexpectedly, the earliest winners of this "contest" were the featured architectures of resorts in popular destinations; these were seldom designed by famous architects.

In 2018, touring guide blog Big Seven Media listed the most "Instagrammable" places in fifty countries that include architecture.[6] Although some famous names—like the Sydney Opera House and the Great Sphinx of Giza—are on the list, the majority of the selection are not architectural masterpieces, but more featured "touristic" architecture. The island of Santorini is one example. It was ruined by an earthquake in 1956 and was later reconstructed in a tourism-oriented neo-vernacular style, which applied the conspicuous dome roofs that Santorini is known for to every hotel room and also added swimming pools (Figure 2). The effect of this reconstruction was prominent and led to Santorini becoming one of the most popular tourist islands beginning in the 1970s. Around the 2010s, the white-and-blue cliff housing clusters were labeled "the most Instagrammable place." A similar pattern was seen with the rainbow-colored terrace houses in Burano Island in Venice (Figure 3).

In some instances, failed architecture has also won popularity. An abandoned unfinished building on the coast of Xia'men, China, which implies no intended development, has also come to be known as an Instagrammable place (Figure 4). Its bareness, hollowness, calmness, and sea backdrop, coincidentally, make this abandoned building a perfect background for portrait photography.

1.4 Development: Participation of Design Architects and Developers

This new, unconventional route to "success" has some architects, especially the "Internet generation" who started their business after 1990, actively designing for Insta-popularity. It has been noted that architects have become more interested in playing with scales and shapes to attract attention. Bjarke Ingels Group (BIG) is a leader of this trend.[7] With their featured design approach of "diagrammatic architecture," BIG translates architecture directly from diagrams (Figure 5). Their buildings, or "built icons," are simple, striking, and easy to understand; such features fit well in mobile-based self-media (Figure 6).

Thomas Heatherwick is potentially another Insta-successful architect. His design is rich in form and sometimes has mobility. His latest project, Vessel, was recommended by some tourist media as the most Insta-worthy place in the Hudson Yards area of Manhattan (Figure 7). In a Sotheby's article, Tom Morris suggests that this could have been because its myriad of viewpoints and reflective skin may have encouraged visitors to interact with it through a smartphone. Heatherwick himself was, however, dismissive of this, stressing the potential that Vessel has to "lift people up," both literally and metaphorically.[8] In this case, the stakeholder that was most eager about Instafamous architecture was the developer, The Related Companies, L.P. As part of its land property project Hudson Yards Development, Vessel contributes to the mission to gain internet flow for the whole project and facilitate business success.

MVRDV Architects (MVRDV) has also designed Instafamous projects that match those of BIG's and Heatherwick's. Big Seven Media (n.d.) ranked their project Markthal Rotterdam in Rotterdam's city center among the top three most Instagrammable places in Rotterdam.[9] Their Tianjin Binhai Library has also won great popularity in the Chinese mobile-based self-media, Weibo. Compared to Heatherwick, who tries to keep a distance from his Insta-popularity, MVRDV seems more accepting and open to being Instafamous. Related Instagram posts on their projects are pinned on MVRDV's official website as part of the project introduction (Figure 8). There are also links to "share one's love" for the project via various self-media.

This embracing attitude is also seen in the design rendering of their Taipei Twin Tower project, which includes the image of someone taking a photo of this colorful cube-stacking tower with a tablet (Figure 9). The rendered scene implies the architect's expectation: to make the tower an Instagrammable landmark.

Markthal Rotterdam wraps more than 200 housing units over an indoor food market (Figure 10). The ceiling painting of chromatic fruits and vegetables is visible at a distance, especially in the evening, making the architecture itself a signboard. Founder Winy Mass's self-evaluation of his work elaborates that the architecture explains its functions directly to a viewer without the need for any pre-existing knowledge of its function, or the premises.[10] MVRDV's coherent populist ideology from design to branding is clear through these three projects.

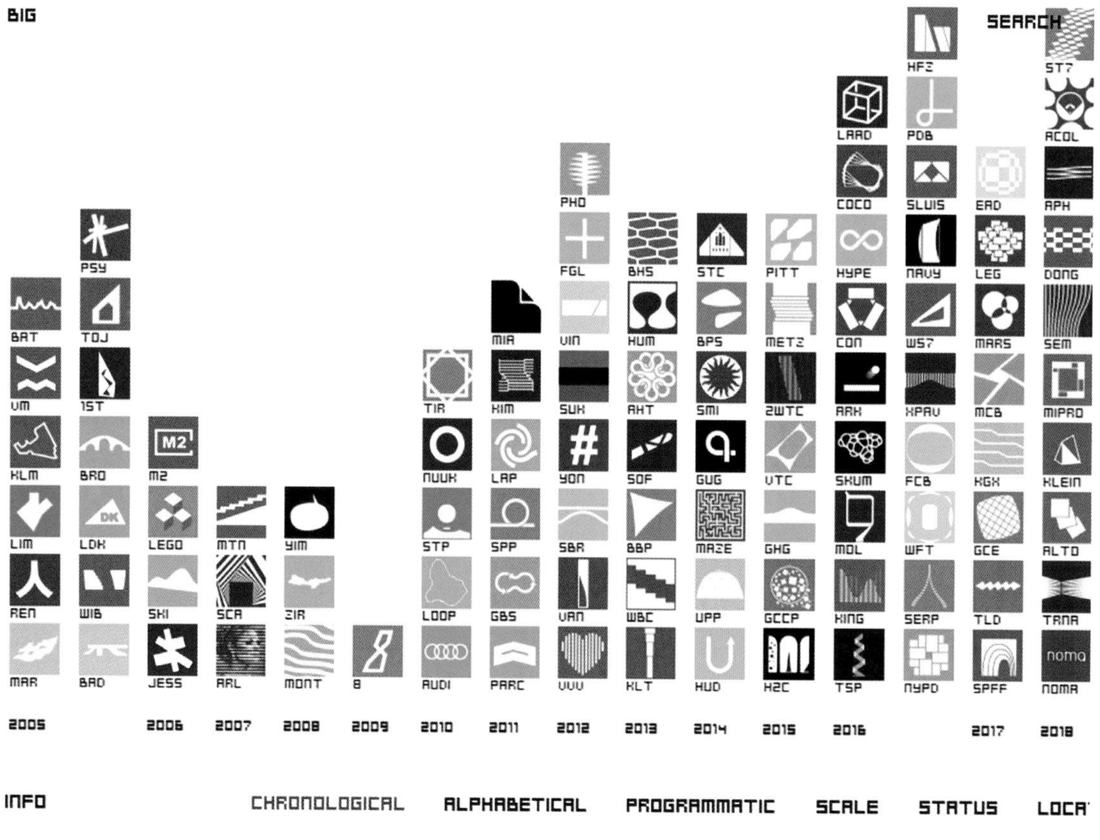

Figure 6
BIG summarizes each project as an icon, which serves as the project catalog on its official website

Figure 7
An Instagram post of Vessel

Figure 8
Pinned Instagram and Twitter posts on MVRDV's official website

1.5 Specialization: Mass Production of Instafamous Architecture

The home renovation reality TV show, *Dream Home*, has also set a new stage in the Instafamous architecture movement (Figure 11). Under the overall plan of a specialized media company, Instafamous architects have been purposely nurtured, and Instafamous architecture has been mass produced.

Produced by Dragon Television in Shanghai, one of the best-known provincial TV stations in China, *Dream Home* was created with a strong ability for resource integration. Every episode, one, or a group of architects, is invited to renovate a house that is in an extremely bad condition; the architect/s is commissioned and paid for by the proprietor. The whole design-construction process is documented and narrated, with an emphasis on the negotiation between clients and architects, and the comparison between "before" and "after" shots of the renovation. Before the episodes air, the *Dream Home* team posts on Weibo and the post is broadly discussed. The official Weibo account of the *Dream Home* series has 1.04 million followers (at the time of writing), which is about triple the number of followers that BIG or MVRDV have on Instagram. The episodes are then broadcast in parallel on Dragon TV, and on online "tubes," such as Aiqiyi, Tencent Video, and LeTV.

The systematic operation successfully produces thirteen Instafamous home renovation projects every year, generating a significant amount of online viewership and discussions; it also effectively incubated a series of Instafamous architects, including Shuhei Aoyama, Yu Ting, and Zhang Hai'ao. With 0.65 million followers on Weibo, Shuhei Aoyama is one of the most famous Japanese architects among the Chinese public.

The projects follow the general design and propagation principles for Instafamous architecture—with eye-catching key

Figure 9
Rendering of Taipei Twin Tower by MVRDV showing a photo capture of the building in a tablet at the bottom right corner

Figure 10
Markthal Rotterdam by MVRDV

Figure 12
Mulan Weichang Tourist Center by HDD Shanghai Huadu Architecture and Urban Design Group, shown in *Dream House*

Figure 11
Captain's House by Vector Architects, shown in *Dream Home*

images (in this case, the before–after comparisons) and catchy nicknames (for example, Home in a Water Tower or A Rockery Home).

Another show in this league of reality home renovation TV shows, and competitor to *Dream Home, is Dream House.* Produced by Zhejiang TV of China, the show adopts a slightly different approach. Instead of exploiting the architects' potential popularity, the show invites celebrities to be the nominal co-designer (Figure 12).

Daniel Wu, a famous movie star from Hong Kong, who also happens to have a bachelor's degree in architecture from the University of Oregon, was selected as the host for the show. He was also the nominal co-designer of Mulan Weichang Visitor Center, which was one of the most popular online architecture projects in China in 2017. As at June 2018, the Center (also designed as a library in the lobby area) had 0.79 million Google search results and over 730 Wechat articles that had been read by over a hundred million users in total. This was not because of Wu's design contribution—that part was conceptualized by HDD Shanghai HuaDu Architecture and Urban Design Group. However, Wu did enhance the viewing experience by triggering the audience's imagination, by showing "the other side of a film star: doing architectural design," which had a decisive appeal to the audience.[11]

Through this new stage, previous leaders of Instafamous architecture were usurped by specialized media companies and the capital funding them. Their emphasis transferred from "using self-media to make Instafamous architecture" to "using the event of architecture design to incubate Instafamous internet profiles and gain internet flow." Unsurprisingly, the Instafamous architects of these two TV shows, inevitably, became even more famous than their projects.

2. Synthesis

2.1 Definition

By tracing the incubation–formation–development process of Instafamous architecture, it can be seen that Instafamous architecture was initially a phenomenon by which some architecture with a certain Instagrammable quality won self-media popularity. Later, it expanded to include a set of design and propagation methods designed to gain internet flow, some of which were transplanted from wild-grown projects.

In the larger picture of the relationships between mass media and modern architecture, we can confirm the position of Instafamous architecture as a new chapter of modern architecture history: on the branch of "architecture and media," and next to "Le Corbusier modernism" and post-modern narrative architecture. It extends the tradition, which modern architecture has used historically to associate with the latest media type, into the self-media era.

2.2 Typology

Through their development stages and their motivations, Instafamous architecture can be classified into three coexisting types: the "wild-grown", the "architect and proprietor driven," and the "media driven." Most wild-grown types were designed before the self-media era, in many cases by the owners and builders, and without the intention of becoming Instafamous. Abandoned unfinished Instafamous buildings—although they might have been built in the Instagram era—are also classified as "wild" because their current condition was not foreseen by their designers.

The architect- and proprietor-driven types were mostly developed by commercial developers and designed by the internet-generation

Figures 13 and 14
The disguised longlines of the Lonely Coastal Library designed by Dong Gong

star-architects, for instance MVRDV, BIG, MAD, and Heatherwick Studio. Either these architects intend to make Instafamous architecture, or their experimental practices collude with the proprietor's endeavor to win internet flow. These projects mostly appear as "built icons."

The media-led types often seem to alienate architecture. For this type, architecture becomes a pure media tool. The built result, though sometimes popular, becomes secondary to the design–construction story and the Instafamous internet profile of the architect.

2.3 Instruments

On the five aspects of building (form, context, color, theme, and naming), we found common design and propagation methods among Instafamous architecture. From the wild-grown Santorini cliff houses, to the LEGO House, and Vessel, there is always mass repetition of a geometrical element. The most common geometrical elements are boxes, spheres (or semi-spheres), and lines (for example, straight-run-stairs), all easily readable by the amateur. The repetition of such elements not only enable panelized prefabrication, but, more importantly, also makes the whole architecture instantly recognizable. Such repetition is also believed to be a powerful tool to create high-quality graphics.

Context is also taken into consideration for the graphic-oriented composition. The domed chapel of Santorini, the Xia'men abandoned building, and Captain's House from *Dream Home*, and the Lonely Coastal Library are all located on deserted coasts. Similarly, Mulan Weichang Visitor Center stands in the middle of an empty steppe; in that vein, the forest location of the Shrine of Whatslove by Wutopia Lab was chosen after the installation was constructed. The sea, steppe, or forest echo the audience's imagination of a distant utopia and provide a clean and textured background for architectural images. This foreground–background hierarchy is emphasized as a principle for graphic design. Moreover, a homogeneous site frees architects from dealing with contextual relationship and enables simplicity in form.

Color composition is also featured in many Instafamous projects. High-saturation polychrome or single colors are two common choices. The former is used by Burano Island, LEGO House, Taipei Twin Tower, and the interior of the arch roof of Markthal Rotterdam. The latter is adopted in Santorini, the Xia'men abandoned building, and the interior of Tianjin Binhai Library. The color of these spaces help exude inner calm, and sometimes loneliness—the typical emotion of urbanites. Such contrasting compositions, both highly recognizable, resonate powerfully with the emotional duality of contemporary urbanites.

In terms of building typology, the architects' and proprietors' interventions focused mainly on medium-or large-scale public buildings, which are the traditional realm of publicity. The new trend brought by *Dream Home and Dream House* was the downsizing of Instafamous architecture. Their featured projects are limited in size, with small buildings and little interior design. This trend may have resulted from the weekly frequency of the shows; a seventy-minute show is a desirable span of time to tell the story of the projects.

The theme of Instafamous architecture also tends to focus on "refreshed low culture." Markthal celebrates the cheap food culture of Rotterdam, evaluated as unashamedly populist. Holding a similar view, architects invited by *Dream Home* tried, at least theoretically, to provide an opportunity at a dignified life in a small space for all inhabitants, even the people's cats.

Analogical nicknames, too, are no longer a taboo for Instagram-decade architecture. The nicknames work well as

Instagram hashtags, and as demotic keywords to introduce and describe the building in a nutshell. For example, the Mulan Weichang Visitor Center is also known as "Daniel Wu's Mongolian Yurt" as it imitates the form of a Mongolian yurt. The name "Vessel New York," which has 195 million search results on Google at March 31, 2019, is much more famous than its official name "Hudson Yards Stairs," which had only 3.62 million Google search results (at March 31, 2019).

Instafamous architecture also sometimes uses exaggerated titles for the sake of publication. The typical formula of these titles is "'the most' + adjective + project type + place;" for example, "the most beautiful bookstore in Suzhou," "the loneliest library in China," "the first carbon fiber architecture in China," or "the most libidinal building in China." For readers, such titles trigger curiosity and attract attention. However, "the loneliest library of China" is not necessarily as "lonely" as its title makes it out to be. Just behind the library—often not exposed on TV or self-media—exists the large neighborhood, Ayana; the library is actually part of this neighborhood (Figures 13 and 14).

3. Multi-Disciplinary Theoretical Relationships

Sometimes, Instafamous architecture is seen to have little merit because it colludes with self-media, succumbs to popular photography, and compromises orthodox values—functionality, materiality, and poetic or technical aesthetics. Some scholars condemned MVRDV's projects for being superficial: "too limited content that could be read up within 20 seconds." However, an Instafamous project is never solitary. It is an inevitable product of a certain zeitgeist. Marketing and communication studies might help explain this inevitability.

3.1 Architecture as Consumer Goods

The industrialized 20th century gave birth to consumerism. Before this, the main task of producers and retailers was catering to the needs of the consumer and competing with their peers to give better quality and service. However, consumerism's mass production led to over-production, and stimulating consumption and creating specific needs became more effective tools. Since the 1950s, planned obsolescence, and poor quality and service have been the main themes of this saturated consumer goods markets.[12]

To solve excessive production, consumerist culture began to emphasize the sign-value of a product over its use-value. As retailers depicted the dreams of every social class, they also spared no effort to associate their products with those dreams, often giving the illusion of approaching them through fanciful pursuits—like eating "middle-class food," such as avocado, buying the latest iPhone each year, or even decorating their homes with Insta-styled furniture. (This consumption gives consumers a "semblance of authority" over their daily lives.)[13]

Hence, people's intentions for visiting and posting about places like Markthal, Vessel, and the Loneliest Library is regarded with suspicion. Are they truly seeking better food than what's in the normal market, or are they simply more attracted by "the sign of food-heaven?" Are they in fact climbing the stairs to a destination, or do they just want to feel "the sense of an elite neighborhood?" Are they genuinely using the seaside library as a reading space, or more as a symbol of escaping from the city?

For real estate development, the new trend is to use Instafamous architecture to add sign-value to the whole project. For the Instafamous architecture in the TV shows mentioned earlier, their sign-value also exceeds their use-value. They share almost all features of consumer goods, except that they are not directly for sale. However, if we take "public attention" as a type of currency, these Instafamous architecture projects have already achieved a remarkable sales volume.

3.2 Architecture as a Stimulator for Consumption

The traditional relationship where the consuming market serves an auxiliary tool for citizens has been inverted. Post-modern cities, especially the contemporary ones, are, in essence, the context for consumption. Nowadays, public life, especially in the new Asian cities that were built on tabula rasa, is mostly carried out in commercial complexes, rather than in traditional public spaces, such as plazas, riverside squares, churches, or temples. To stimulate consumption, these complexes try to create a sense of dreamland where the consumers get the "semblance of authority." The further from reality, the more dreamlike the experience becomes. The stronger the feeling of "escape into another world" consumers get, the higher the possibility they might purchase something. *Coney Island*, written by Koolhaas, could be an early example. Owing to a "reality shortage" in New York, surreal amusement parks were built on Coney Island as tourist destinations for New Yorkers.[14] Disneyland is the contemporary version of Coney Island. According to Steven Miles, Disneyland is actually a mall, where the structures are carefully designed to encourage consumption, in addition to visiting the park.[15]

The Chinese bookstore chain, Zhongshuge, known on self-media as "the most beautiful bookshop," adopted such a method in its design. Architect Yu Ting undertook the interior design of two of their stores in Suzhou and Xi'an (Figures 15 and 16). Both stores carefully adopt Instafamous color schemes: the Suzhou store with a rainbow-colored ceiling and the Xi'an store with a pure white interior that highlights the chromatic book covers. They create a "wonder space" which is far removed from people's usual experiences of bookstores, targeted toward stimulating consumers to make actual purchases (more than normal) beyond just browsing.

3.3 Architecture in "the World as a Picture"

The way modern people understand the world has been fundamentally changed by the synergy of both consumerism and the evolution of image-based media. Martin Heidegger, a German philosopher of the 20th century, pointed out that when a picture is understood essentially, it does not mean a picture of the world.[16] Instead, it is the real world that is grasped as a picture. This trend has intensified in the 2010s—the decade of self-media. On the one hand, the information barrier between every individual, business, and institution has been broken. On the other hand, information sharing has become highly formalized into fragmented pictures with limited text. This form also applies to online purchasing platforms.

Thus, the public might have started to consider everything and everyone, including every piece of architecture, as a picture. Consequently, vibrant colors, mass repetitious composition, and pure backgrounds that help to make an attractive picture, become important architectural languages. More complex stories, including poetics, tectonics, and context are not easy to deliver through self-media and thus may be relatively weakened.

Even future architects may not escape from this overwhelming "kingdom of mass media." Where 20th-century architecture students started case studies from a book, a magazine, a lecture, or a real visit, the 21st-century students are more likely to begin with *Archdaily*, *Dezeen* or Pinterest. The tendency toward visualism and formalism is

Figure 15
Zhongshuge bookstore interior, Suzhou

Figure 16
Zhongshuge bookstore interior, Xi'an

thus embedded and inevitable. Therefore, it is reasonable that the popularity of Instafamous architecture will be most prominent in China, the 2010s' largest mobile-internet market and real estate market.

3.4 Architects' Success Through "Populism"

The popularization of self-media, together with the global economic downturn after 2008, has led to the resurgence of populism. Even the monopolization of elite politicians has been broken by media stars. Neither Donald Trump nor Volodymyr Zelensky had any political experience before their election. However, they became popular through Twitter, and TV programs/comedies, which greatly helped their success. Populists appeal to "the people" by acting against "the elites." They are also skilled in using "bad manners" to prove themselves to be one of "the people."

A similar trend is seen in the architectural realm. Mass media enables everyone to participate in architectural criticism. The previous monopolized authority of star-architects, scholars, and associations has become impaired. Being Instafamous provides an alternative way for architects, especially those without many social resources, to win popularity.

The correlation between the age of star-architects or architectural firms and their attitude toward Instafamous architecture confirms this. The star-architects and offices who were famous before 2000 seem to be indifferent toward the Instafamous phenomenon. They tend to continue their prominent personal styles or design manifestos.

Younger star-architects, such as MVRDV, BIG, Heatherwick Studio, and MAD, who became famous in the early internet age between 2000 and 2010, seem to fit into the age of mass media automatically. They can be defined as Instafamous-adapting architects. Many of their works became Instafamous, although this wasn't their main intention. Ma Yansong, founder of MAD, showed some antipathy toward media-oriented architectural practice, stressing the personal pursuit of architecture. However, he also sees mass media as an available tool for delivering his own ideas. Instafamous-adapting architects are skilled in attention catching and storytelling. At the same time as insisting on their own philosophy, they also welcome the epoch, and are conversely welcomed.

The third group, including Zhang Hai'ao, Yu Ting, Zhuang Ziyu, and Shuhei Aoyama are, so-called, proactive Instafamous architects. They were not famous before the popularization of self-media, yet they won instant renown the first time they participated in *Dream Home*. The immaturity of the Chinese star-architect system gives them this chance. Zhang Hai'ao claimed to use broadcasting as a shortcut to being famous. In his opinion, the Instafamous architect is the one whose design appeals to the masses.[17]

3.5 People's Mind Shift in the Self-Media Era

Since the prevalence of television, concentration and deep, critical thinking have become scarcer among the population. The television, internet, and now, self-media provide free and convenient knowledge to everyone. However, as indicated by Neil Postman, author and media theorist, television must make any information, idea, and story directly understandable, in case it causes perplexity and fails to keep the audience's attention.[18] The principal target is the learner's contentment, rather than their authentic growth. Compared with television, internet information might be even shallower and more distractive. Nicholas Carr describes the internet as "no Sleepy Hollow."[19] The ubiquitous information fragments exhaust the audience's attention, without giving them a chance for contemplation. The city itself has been the accomplice of

Figures 17 and 18
"Before and after" images of a renovation in the urban village of Guangzhou by URBANUS that was featured in *Dream Home*

media-driven mind shifts. According to Berman, Jonides, and Kaplan, the level of cognitive control can be increased substantially by interacting with nature.[20] Thus the mega-city residents who are detached from nature are more easily distracted.

Most people seldom escape from this overwhelming world of internet and media. With a somewhat pessimistic attitude, architects might have no choice but to design superficial architecture when the mind of the public has been shaped to enjoy superficial things.

4. Evaluation

Having established the historical framework and theoretical relationships of Instafamous architecture, we now evaluate the values and risks of Instafamous architecture through the perspective of history, socio-economics, and culture.

4.1 Value 1: The Unity of Commercial Benefit, Public Interest, and Architect Aspirations

In the past, the economic benefits of commercial developers, the public interest, and architect aspirations seldom reached total agreement. The developers desired higher efficiency, the public sought novelty, but was afraid of peculiarity, while the architects sought every chance to play with design. When the architect's opinion conflicted with the developer, the developer usually won. Architects might occasionally win by "pushing it right through," like Louis Kahn, who was highly appreciated by the profession, but at the expense of his own bankruptcy. When a pioneering architectural design was not understood by the public—though it may be accepted and praised by the public decades later, such as Gustave Eiffel's Eiffel Tower, Sir Peter Cook's Kunsthaus Graz, I. M. Pei's expansion of the Louvre Museum, and Rem Koolhaas' CCTV Tower—the reputation of that architect and the authority of the architectural profession may be damaged at that time.

In Instafamous architecture, we might have found a way to balance those contradictory values. In these projects, developers benefit from drawing more public attention and visitors, and this offers architects the chance to challenge regularity and create new designs, as well as to increase their own popularity. Moreover, as the developers build projects such as Vessel or the Loneliest Library on their commercial land, and make them free for entry, they are adding public facilities to the city.

4.2 Value 2: Bringing Attention and Flow to Architectural Issues

As a powerful media tool, Instafamous architecture can bring public attention and internet flow to certain architectural issues, such as rural village revitalization and urban village regeneration.

During rapid urbanization in the early 21st century, Chinese rural villages were hollowed-out. With most of the working population migrating to cities, resulting in considerable loss of cultural identity, rural villages are currently struggling to recover from continuous recession, despite financial aid from the government for infrastructure developments. The Instafamous Mulan Weichang Visitor Center was referred to by its designer, Zhang Hai'ao, as an acupuncture therapy for this dilemma. With this single Instafamous architecture project, minimal environmental impact, and a total construction cost of 1 million RMB (around $US 155,000), the village now attracts a large number of visitors, which has increased the villagers' income.[21] In parallel, the building also raised the public's awareness of the place and triggered related discussions.

Similar stories have happened in urban villages, for instance, in Shenzhen, China. The projects in the pilot episode of *Dream Home* helped to set up a model of designing for decency in high-density and low-income areas (Figures 17 and 18). and also helped raise social awareness of the urban village problem.

Further, by introducing these topics to the public for their responses, Instafamous architects maintain the influence of architecture in the distracting world of media and consumerism, where the separation between architects and the public has been broken down.

4.3 Risk 1: Producing Low-quality Architecture

Instafamous architecture is "space-less." Professor D. J. Rosbottom expressed concern that the over-privileging of the visual relationship between humans and architecture would degrade architecture from a place "to encounter and experience, and to situate people in the world," to hardly anything more than an object.[22] The way that people react with Instafamous architecture is mainly visual. They make "favorite" and mark Instafamous spots by sorting images. They prove they have visited locations by snapping selfies in front of a project and sharing them. Through such a fast-paced loop, visitors miss the chance to experience the space and interact with local people. This makes some Instafamous architecture more likely a pure object, without the variety of spontaneous narratives that sustains its cultural vitality.

Instafamous architecture can also lack utility and durability, which does not affect their short-term popularity. Since it aims to merely deliver "a sense," which could either be a sense of a certain type of lifestyle, the desire to consume, or a sense of humanistic care, the usage scenario is less important. *Dream House* has been accused by some proprietors of creating poor utility and bad construction quality. It was even reported on Sohu.com, an online service and news provider, that a proprietor on *Dream House* had complained that his renovated home had become "a sound stage," which was far from what he needed.[23] When designing the room for his aged, seriously ill mother, the design team used a board-fabricated bed, with only a thin mattress. A row of skylights was also designed in an unheated washroom, resulting in poor thermal preservation in winter.

4.4 Risk 2: Reducing the Content of the Architectural Profession

The dual character of self-media contains both the broad coverage of audience and participants and the limited size of information transferred. To remain influential, Instafamous architecture has to keep its size small, its concept understandable, and its functionality close enough to daily life. By watching television shows and reading self-media posts, people learn about architecture as icons of amusement. As Postman describes, they might feel an illusory sense of gaining knowledge although the knowledge is too shallow to be reliable.[24] This might limit the audience's understanding of architectural design to small-scale, context-less, function-less buildings, and their illustrated, colorful, material-less key images, which does not correctly represent the profession.

Although this might not influence higher architectural education, there is a risk that young architecture students will form a prejudiced mindset before university, influenced by the overwhelming media-based architectural knowledge. In the long run, this might result in the loss of architectural culture and be described as "amusing architecture to death."

4.5 Risk 3: Unsustainable and Unreproducible Attention and Flow

The attention of the public is limited and ever-shifting (Figure 19). Instafamous architecture projects may become an overnight sensation, however, their popularity also fades away just as quickly. An Instafamous architecture might bring instant fame to a hollowed-out village, but it cannot stop the village from later being forgotten.

Adding to that—because the way that Instafamous architecture brings attention to a single village is to concentrate on it—this results in the majority of other villages possibly becoming even more neglected. Zhang Hai'ao himself also pointed out that the Mulan

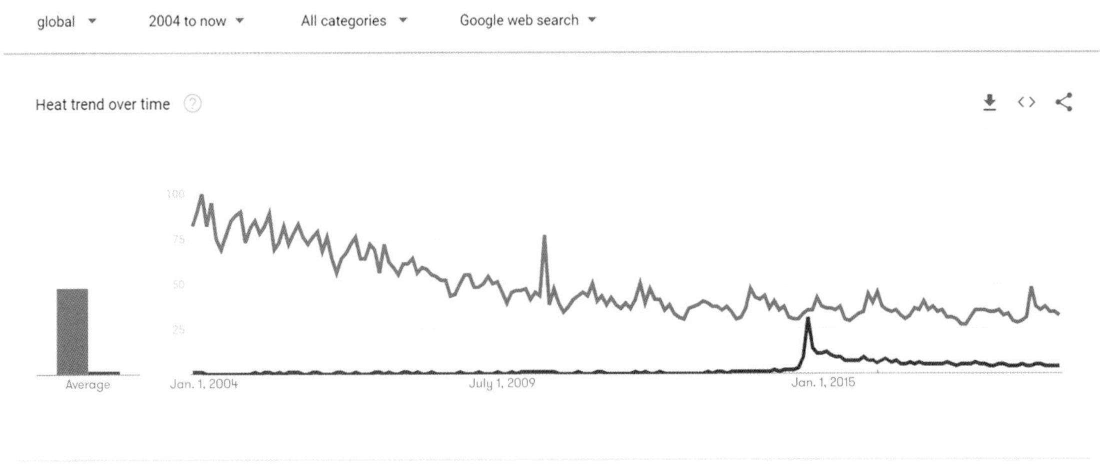

Figure 19
Google Trends comparison between Markthal Rotterdam (red line, representing Instafamous architecture) and Sydney Opera House (blue line, representing a classical architectural masterpiece)

Weichang project should be regarded only as a leverage point rather than a universal solution to the entire rural village problem.

4.6 Contradictory: Architecture of the Spirit in the Self-media Age

Zeitgeist, or the spirit of time, has become an appreciated notion since the time of Georg Hegel, a German philosopher, and is stressed by the modernists. Pioneer architect Louis Sullivan advocates that architecture should be an expression and an outcome of certain conditions in a civilization, rather than a style.[25] A similar manifesto was put forth by German architect Ludwig Mies van der Rohe, that architecture should express the will of the age. We can see the architectural creations of Sullivan and Mies as the expression of more efficient production in the early industrialized society. Instafamous architecture today expresses the will to stimulate and continuously satisfy the desire for consumption, as well as presents the aspiration for more efficient communication, both of which belong to the contemporary context. This confirms the significance of Instafamous architecture as a new chapter of architectural history.

However, could the "spirit of time" still represent justice? When the modernists advocated for zeitgeist, they believed that the new technology and production would initiate new culture and add to the existing culture. From "form follows function" to "form follows fiction," and then to high-tech architecture and digital architecture, the 20th century's architectural movements have kept chasing the zeitgeist and kept increasing the meaning of architecture.

The neutrality of technology and its relationship with culture during the early modern time has already been fundamentally changed. Mobile-internet technologies may possibly lead to a culture decay by over simplifying it. For the first time in modern history, architects struggle to choose between following the spirit of time and protecting the architectural culture from decaying; supporters of the former are dismissed by the latter as "Instafamous architects."

Without ecstatic welcoming, or distasteful avoidance, but with ambivalence, we regard Instafamous architecture as the spirit of the self-media age.

5. Conclusion

This thesis has traced the incubation, formation, and development process of the Instafamous architecture genre, aimed to define and classify it, and discussed its inevitability by finding multidisciplinary theoretical relationships. It has helped to establish the historical and theoretical framework of this architectural movement, supplementing the "missing chapter" of modern architectural history and also enabling Instafamous architecture to be analyzed and evaluated, rather than be avoided or dismissed by the profession. The thesis has also provided its own evaluation of Instafamous architecture, which is of dual character and is contradictory. It suggests that the profession should stay aware and critical of this "architecture of the self-media age."

Notes

1. Rem Koolhaas, *Delirious New York: a Retroactive Manifesto for Manhattan* (New York: The Monacelli Press, 2014), 61.
2. Beatriz Colomina, *Privacy and Publicity: Modern Architecture as Mass Media* (Woburn, Massachusetts: MIT Press, 1996), 5–14.
3. *Metropolis*, 1927; directed by Fritz Lang, Universum Film A.G., Babelsberg, https://www.youtube.com/watch?v=OZ_mcUz8hkQ.
4. Christoph Meinel and Harald Sack, *Digital Communication: Communication, Multimedia, Security* (Heielberg: Springer, 2014).
5. "Holiday Destination Chosen Based on How 'Instagrammable' the Holiday Pics Will Be," Schofields Insurance Ltd., last modified April 3, 2017, https://www.schofields.ltd.uk/blog/5123/two-fifths-of-millennials-choose-their-holiday-.
6. "The 7 Most Instagrammable Spots in Rotterdam," Big Seven Travel, last modified November 19, 2018, https://bigseventravel.com/7-most-instagrammable-spots-rotterdam/.
7. Bella Mackie, "Is Instagram Changing The Way We Design The World," *The Guardian*, July 12, 2018, https://www.theguardian.com/lifeandstyle/2018/jul/12/ready-for-your-selfie-why-public-spaces-are-being-insta-designed.
8. Tom Morris, "Thomas Heatherwick's Eye-Catching New Structure Is a Vessel for Change," *Sotheby's Magazine*, February 14, 2019, https://www.sothebys.com/en/articles/thomas-heatherwicks-eye-catching-vessel-structure-in-new-yorks-hudson-yards.
9. Big Seven Travel, "Instagrammable Spots."
10. Rob Bevan, "Market Hall in Rotterdam by MVRDV," *Architectural Review*, January 5, 2015, https://www.architectural-review.com/today/markthal-in-rotterdam-by-mvrdv.
11. Yang Yu, "Architecture as Media Blockbuster: Mulan Weichang Library," *Time + Architecture*, 4 (2018): 110–119.
12. George S. Day and David A. Aaker, "Marketing Education: A Guide to Consumerism," *Journal of Marketing* 34, no. 3 (1970): 12–19.
13. Steven Miles, *Consumerism: As a Way of Life*. (London: SAGE Publications, 1998), 25.
14. Koolhaas, *Delirious New York*, 77.
15. Miles, *Consumerism: As a Way of Life*, 65.
16. Martin Heidegger, *The Question Concerning Technology and Other Essays* (New York & London: Garland Publishing, 1977), 3.
17. Zhang Hai'ao, "Net-flow is Just a Phenomenon: What are Architects Doing No. 136," *Archiposition*, April 20, 2019, https://www.archiposition.com/items/20190420105535.
18. Neil Postman, *Amusing Ourselves to Death: Public Discourse in the Age of Show Business* (Penguin Books, 2006), 147.
19. Nicholas Carr, *The Shallows: What the Internet is Doing to Our Brain* (New York: W.W. Norton & Company, 2010), 34.
20. Marc G. Berman, John Jonides, and Stephen Kaplan, "The Cognitive Benefits of Interacting with Nature," *Psychological Science* 19, no. 12 (2008): 1207–1212.
21. Hai'ao, Zhang, "Media Influence on Rural Construction: A Case Study of Mulan Weichang Visitor Centre," *Architecture Technologies*, no. 5 (2018), 66–73.
22. Daniel Rosbottom, "Towards a Congruent Architecture" in *Delft Lectures on Architectural Design Edition 2015/2016*, ed., Susanne Komossa et al., TU Delft Open, 2018, 151–166, https://books.bk.tudelft.nl/index.php/press/catalog/book/isbn.9789463660815.
23. Wang Yan, "Dream Home by Oriental TV: A Shoddy Show," Sohu.com, last modified January 12, 2017, http://www.sohu.com/a/124149973_584217.
24. Heidegger, *The Question Concerning Technology and Other Essays*, 35.
25. Joseph Siry, *Carson Pirie Scott: Louis Sullivan and the Chicago Department Store*, (Chicago: University of Chicago Press, 1988), 240.

Figure Credits

Figure 1: Ustad Ahmad Lahauri, Taj Mahal, Uttar Pradesh, 1914, photographed by Helen Messinger Murdoch, cited in *National Geographic*, https://en.wikipedia.org/wiki/Helen_Messinger_Murdoch#/media/File:Taj_Mahal_1921.JPG.
Figure 2: An Instagram post on Burano, 2019, posted by @ournextflight.
Figure 3: An Instagram post on Santorini, 2019, posted by @ournextflight.
Figure 4: A collage post on Xiaohongshu highlights the abandoned unfinished building on the coast of Xia'men, China, posted by @李搞笑, @橡树果-, @Tilly Chen, @朝梦夕拾, @陈彦霖Ann.
Figure 5: BIG, LEGO House, Billund, 2021, https://big.dk/#projects-leg (authors' image).
Figure 6: BIG, each project summarized as an icon, 2021, https://big.dk/#projects (authors' image).
Figure 7: Instagram post of Vessel, Manhattan, 2019, posted by @pankratova916.
Figure 8: Pinned Instagram and Twitter posts on MVRDV's official website, 2021, https://mvrdv.nl/projects/246/tianjin-binhai-library (authors' image).
Figure 9: MVRDV, Taipei Twin Tower, Taipei, 2021, https://mvrdv.nl/projects/371/taipei-twin-towers (authors' image).
Figure 10: MVRDV, Markthall Rotterdam, 2021, https://mvrdv.nl/projects/115/markthal (authors' image).
Figure 11: Vector Architects, Captain's House, Fuzhou, 2016, photographed by Hao Chen, https://www.archdaily.cn/cn/871456/chuan-chang-zhi-jia-gai-zao-zhi-xiang-jian-zhu.
Figure 12: HDD Shanghai Huadu Architecture and Urban Design Group, Mulan Weichang Tourist Center, Mulan Weichang, 2016, photographed by Shengliang Su, https://www.archdaily.com/886919/mulan-weichang-vistor-centre-hdd/5a56c486f197cc250900017d-mulan-weichang-vistor-centre-hdd-photo.
Figure 13: Vector Architects, The Lonely Coastal Library, Qinhuangdao, 2015, photographed by Shengliang Su, https://www.archdaily.cn/cn/768089/hai-bian-tu-shu-guan-zhi-xiang-jian-zhu-vector-architects/556d25afe58eceec91000130-seashore-library-vector-architects-photo.
Figure 14: Vector Architects, The Lonely Coastal Library, Qinhuangdao, 2021, https://www.google.com/maps/@39.6593595,119.3249657,759a,35y,243.98h,45.88t/data=!3m1!1e3?hl=zh-CN (Google Map resource).
Figure 15: Wutopia Lab, Zhongshuge bookshop interior in Suzhou, 2017, photographed by CreateAR images, https://www.archdaily.cn/cn/877844/jin-shu-cai-hong-li-de-shu-dian-su-zhou-zhong-shu-ge-wutopia-lab?ad_source=search&ad_medium=search_result_projects.
Figure 16: Wutopia Lab, Zhongshuge bookshop interior in Xi'an, Xi'an, 2018, photographed by CreateAR images, https://www.archdaily.cn/cn/897875/xi-an-zhong-shu-ge-wutopia-lab?ad_source=search&ad_medium=search_result_all.
Figure 17: URBANUS, *Dream Home* renovation in urban village: "before" shot, Guangzhou, 2018, https://www.archdaily.cn/cn/920203/yan-zhou-li-shi-jie-qu-nei-dong-ji-xiao-zhu-zhai-de-gai-zao-da-yin-yu-shi-urbanusdu-shi-shi-jian?ad_name=article_cn_redirect=popup (authors' image).
Figure 18: URBANUS, *Dream Home* renovation in urban village: "after" shot, Guangzhou, 2018, photographed by Chao Zhang, https://www.archdaily.cn/cn/920203/yan-zhou-li-shi-jie-qu-nei-dong-ji-xiao-zhu-zhai-de-gai-zao-da-yin-yu-shi-urbanusdu-shi-shi-jian?ad_name=article_cn_redirect=popup.
Figure 19: Google Trends comparison between Markthal Rotterdam and Sydney Opera House, 2021, https://trends.google.com/trends/explore?date=all&q=%2Fm%2F06_nm,%2Fg%2F11b6j48lmf.

My Montessori Garden

Main façade of the building

Architect firm: HGAA, Vietnam
Principal architect: NGUYỄN Văn Thu
Design team: NGUYỄN Minh Đức, NGUYỄN Văn Tính
Location: Ha Long, Vietnam
Area: 340 square meters
Completion date: December 2018
Photography: Duc NGUYEN

"Montessori" is an education approach that originated in Europe in the early 20th century and it has been developing in Vietnam in recent years. The Montessori approach/method respects the independence of children and creates an environment for children to explore and interact with the world through their own senses.

My Montessori Garden is a Montessori-oriented preschool. The concept is to create a garden—a natural space for children, a classroom between the trees and flowers.

The construction site is located in a residential area in Ha Long City, Quang Ninh, one of the fastest-growing cities in Vietnam. The architects sought to achieve change through the simple, but valuable things that they could do for the children. The current site is located in a fairly densely populated area. Initially, it was an empty lot that was used by local people as a vegetable garden. This inspired the school to create a garden, not only for the kids in the school, but also for the people in the area.

As the land can only be leased for five to ten years, a simple construction structure that could be installed quickly—that would have little impact on the existing land—and which can easily be relocated to another location when needed was the way to go.

Toward this, a steel structure solution was derived, creating two blocks of steel-framed classrooms surrounded by gardens. Outside these two blocks, is a trellis system of steel frame and wire mesh to create two gardens—one with big trees on the ground, and one with fruit vines above—connected by a system of three iron stairs and overhead walkways, forming a continuous cycle of circulation in the garden. Children will have more space to move from the ground to the top and back down, which will make the school an interesting space of discovery. The children can run about, look at the plants, touch them, and watch them grow every day. In this garden, children can learn how to plant and care for fruit vines, seasonal vegetables, and their favorite flowers.

Although the land area is not large—measuring only about 600 square meters—the project's investor was determined to dedicate more than 50 percent of the land to the garden in order to create a learning space close to nature, in which the children would be able to learn, connect, and interact with nature more often than would be possible in regular classes.

In terms of microclimate, the tree garden surrounding the classroom also creates a cool and quiet atmosphere for the classrooms, while creating views and green landscapes for all classes.

To seek change from simple but bold architectural solutions—such as creating a classroom in the middle of a garden right in the heart of the city—the architects hope to contribute to improving the quality of educational spaces, and to inspire the next wave of change.

Aerial view

Layers of trees in the garden

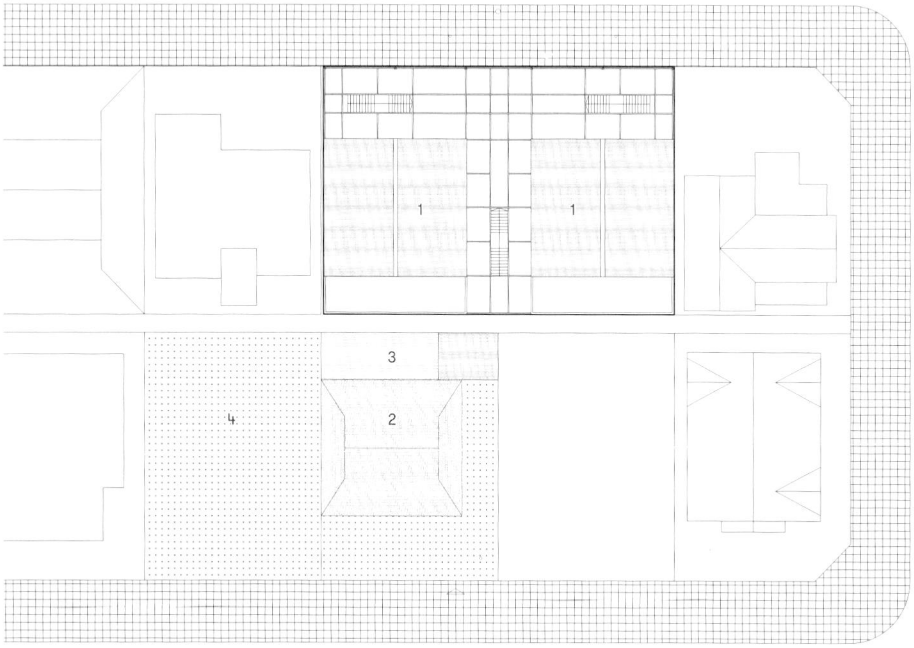

1. My Montessori garden
2. Old kindergarten
3. Kitchen
4. Yard

Site location

Stairs that ascend to the walkway

Another view of the walkway

The space is well-lit with natural light

The classroom space overlooks the garden

Daily activities take place by the garden

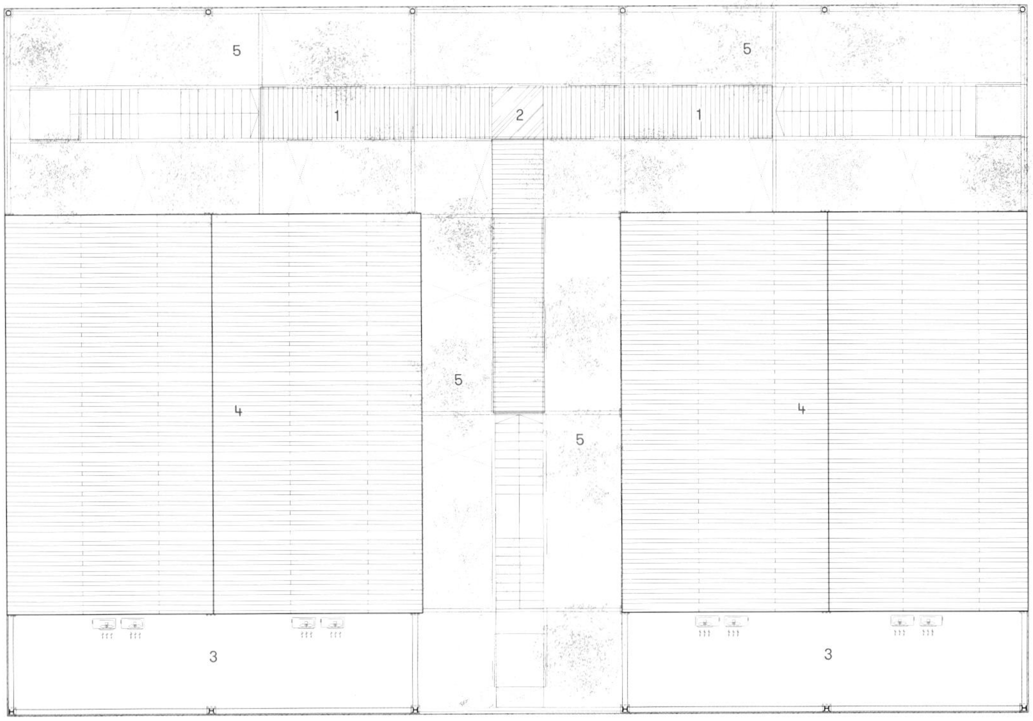

Roof plan

1. Walkway
2. Glass floor
3. Technical floor
4. Classroom block
5. Steel mesh for vine

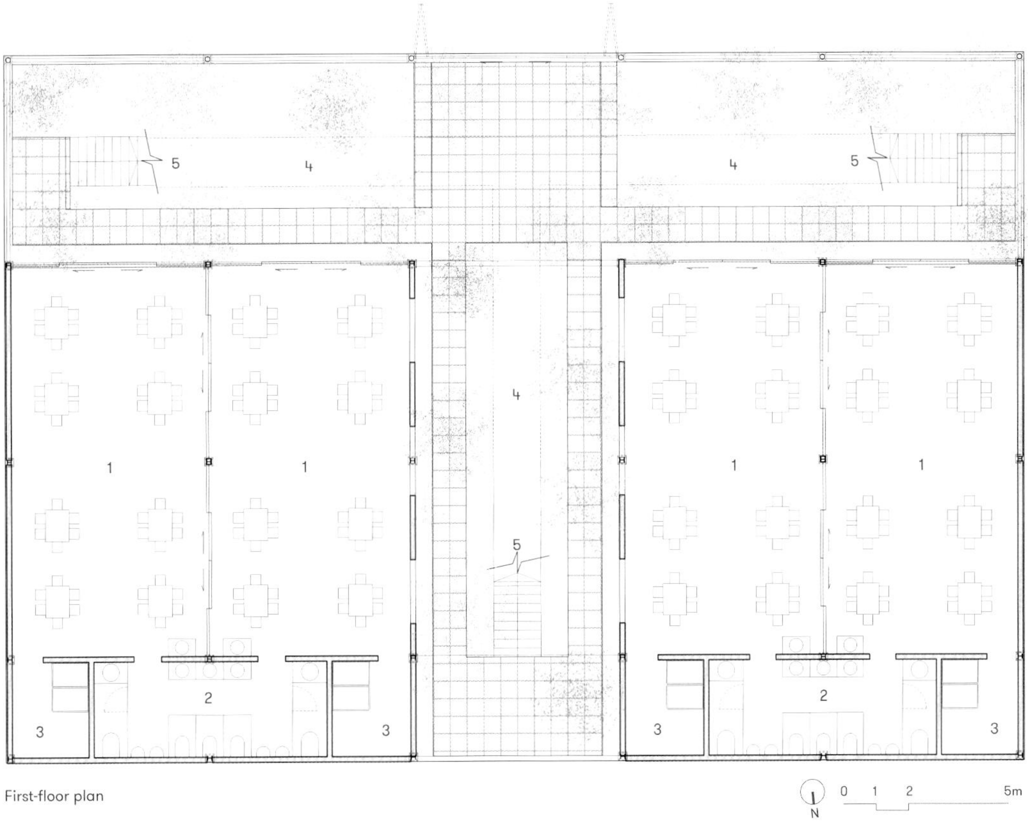

First-floor plan

1. Classroom
2. WC
3. Storage
4. Vegetable garden
5. Stairs

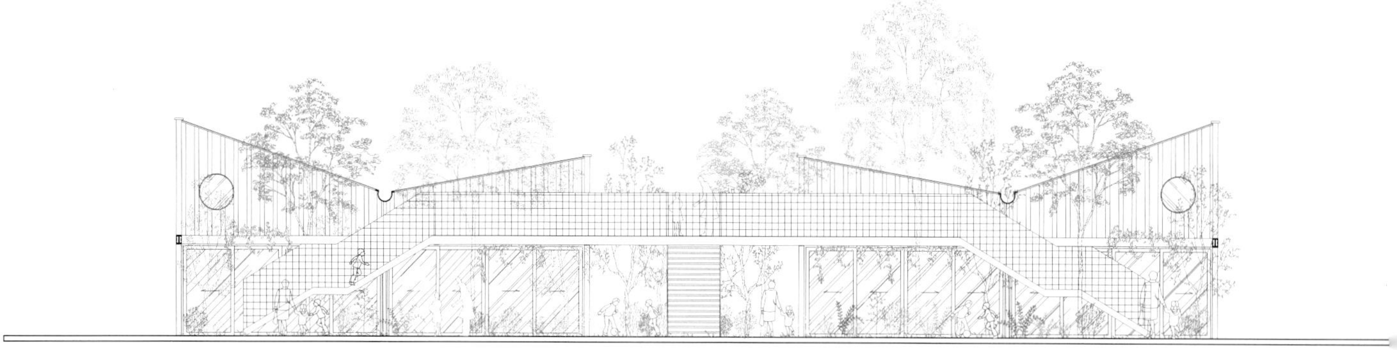

Elevation

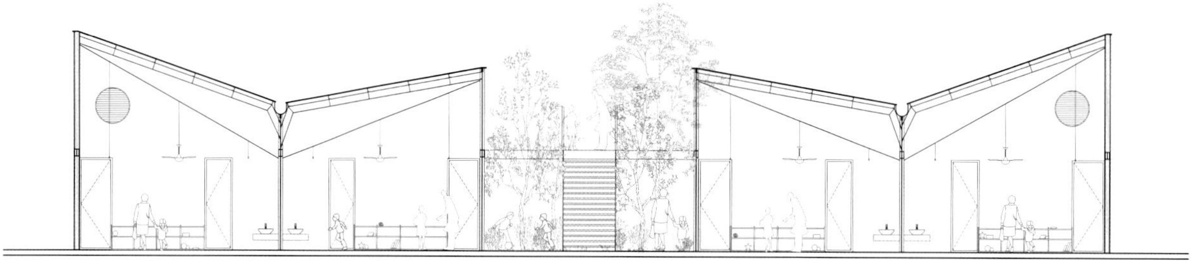

Section 1

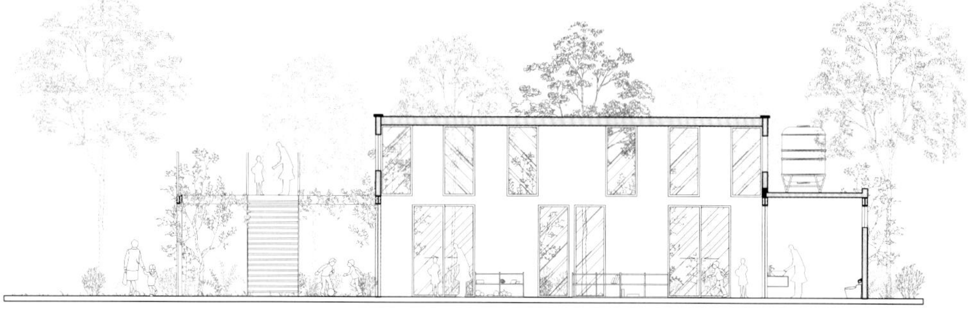

Section 2

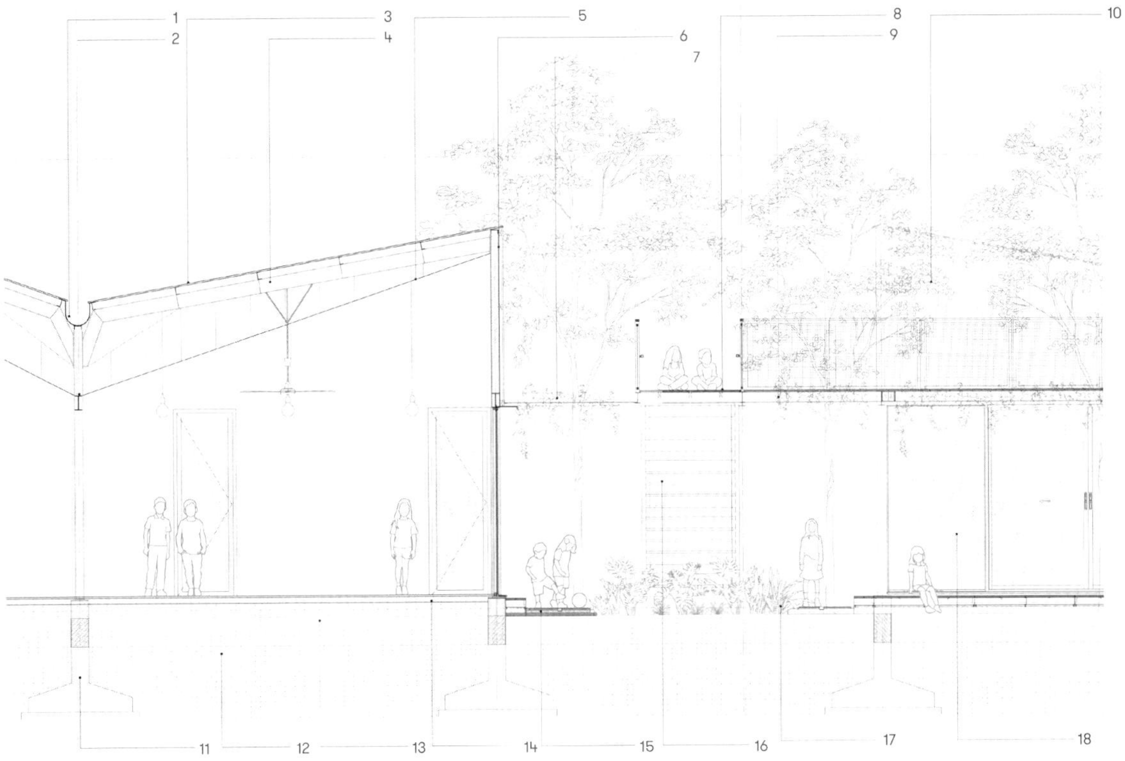

Detail drawing

1. Gutter
2. 1 beam steel H200
3. Corrugated roof with heat insulator
4. Steel truss structure
5. Plaster ceiling with insulator layer
6. Brick wall with corrugated steel cladding
7. Steel mesh for vines
8. Walkways with wooden paving
9. 1 shape steel H150
10. Brick wall with corrugated steel cladding
11. Reinforced-concrete
12. Soil layer
13. Macadam layer
14. Wooden floor
15. Ground pathway
16. Steel stairway
17. Vegetable garden
18. Aluminum glass doors

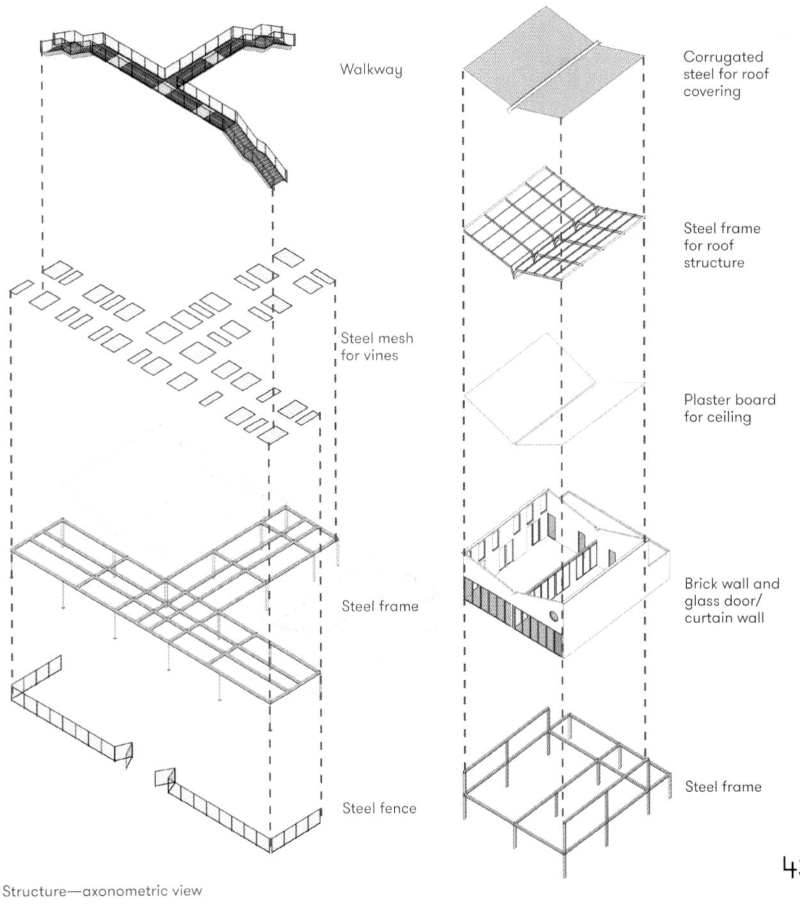

Structure—axonometric view

Fuseika

Exterior — view from the southwest with louvered doors closed

Architect firm: T-Square Design Associates, Japan
Principal architect: Shigeru TSUDA
Design team: Shinsaku KATAOKA
Location: Ashiya City, Japan
Area: 113.96 square meters
Completion date: June 2019
Photography: Shigeo OGAWA

This project is the architect's own residence. It took years to find an ideal site that represents the surrounding area—somewhere that has a meaning. A site in Ashiya City, Hyogo, Japan was sought. The most symbolic signatures of this city are the Yamamura House (now called the Yodoko Guest House), designed by Frank Lloyd Wright, and the Yamaguchi House (now called the Tekisui Museum), designed by Takeo Yasui, one of the most well-known Japanese architects who lived at the same time as Wright; both houses sit nearby to the Ashiya river, known for the beautiful cherry blossom trees that decorate the riverside. These two houses sit across from each other, with the river in between, and they can be seen from the project site. (A perfect site for an architect to build his own house!)

As one of the construction ideas was to not rely on using any cooling system like air conditioning, the site that would eventually be selected had to sit near or by the river to catch the natural wind (river breeze), which would help to cool the house. And so, after a long search, the perfect site was found near the Ashiya river, just between the two symbolic houses, which can be spotted from the site.

Also, three sides of the site are surrounded by roads, making it easier to open the property out to the surroundings to catch the natural wind. This was how the plan started: catch the natural wind to cool the house, and also enjoy a picturesque view of the two iconic architectural structures from the house—this became the main concept of the project.

Designing a house without using any type of electronic cooling system, and which would rely on natural wind seemed like an easy enough task to achieve, but with the hot and humid summer conditions, as well as the high density of houses in Japan, it was very difficult. The architect focused on the building technique and designs of old-style, traditional Japanese houses where no machines were used to cool the house.

A long canopy that often played an important role in controlling sunlight in traditional houses is interpreted into a terrace at the outer rim of the house. This terrace with louvers above is deep enough to temper the summer sunlight and create enough shadow space in the interior. At the outer rim of this terrace, there are louvered sliding doors that control the wind, light, and view. They also act as a double skin for the house and prevent insects and critters from entering. The angle and distance of each blade was very carefully studied by making mockups in order to derive the best angle that would prevent the inhabitants from being seen by their neighbors, while letting natural light into the living space at the same time.

At the inner rim, there are glass sliding doors that physically divide the interior from the exterior. The floor plan was carefully studied so that no walls block the wind-flow within the house. During the summer, the glass doors are kept open and the louvered doors are closed at all times to block out the hot summer sunlight and to let the wind flow. Because the house is wide open in almost all directions, it can sometimes become quite humid within during certain seasons. Therefore, natural wood is used as a finish for the interior walls to control the humidity (the house sits near the river, and it is quite humid inside and outside from early summer to late summer). During the winter, the glass doors are closed and the louvered doors are open at all times to capture the natural sunlight; a hidden heated floor system keeps the interior space warm.

Exterior — night view from the southeast corner

Exterior — view from the east with louvered doors open

Bedroom — the relationship between the bedroom, terrace, and pathway is shown

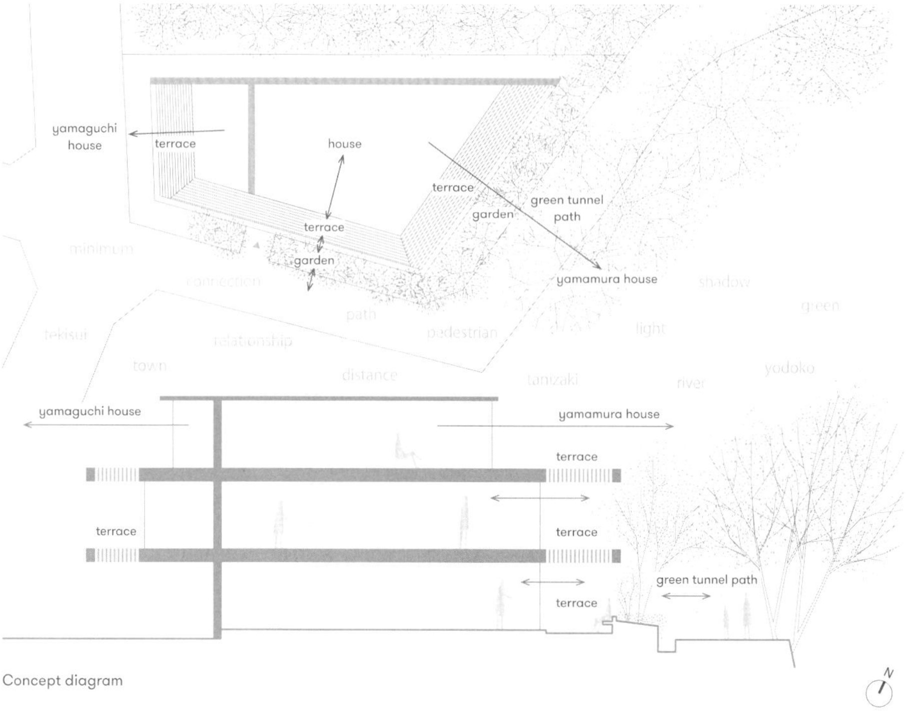

Concept diagram

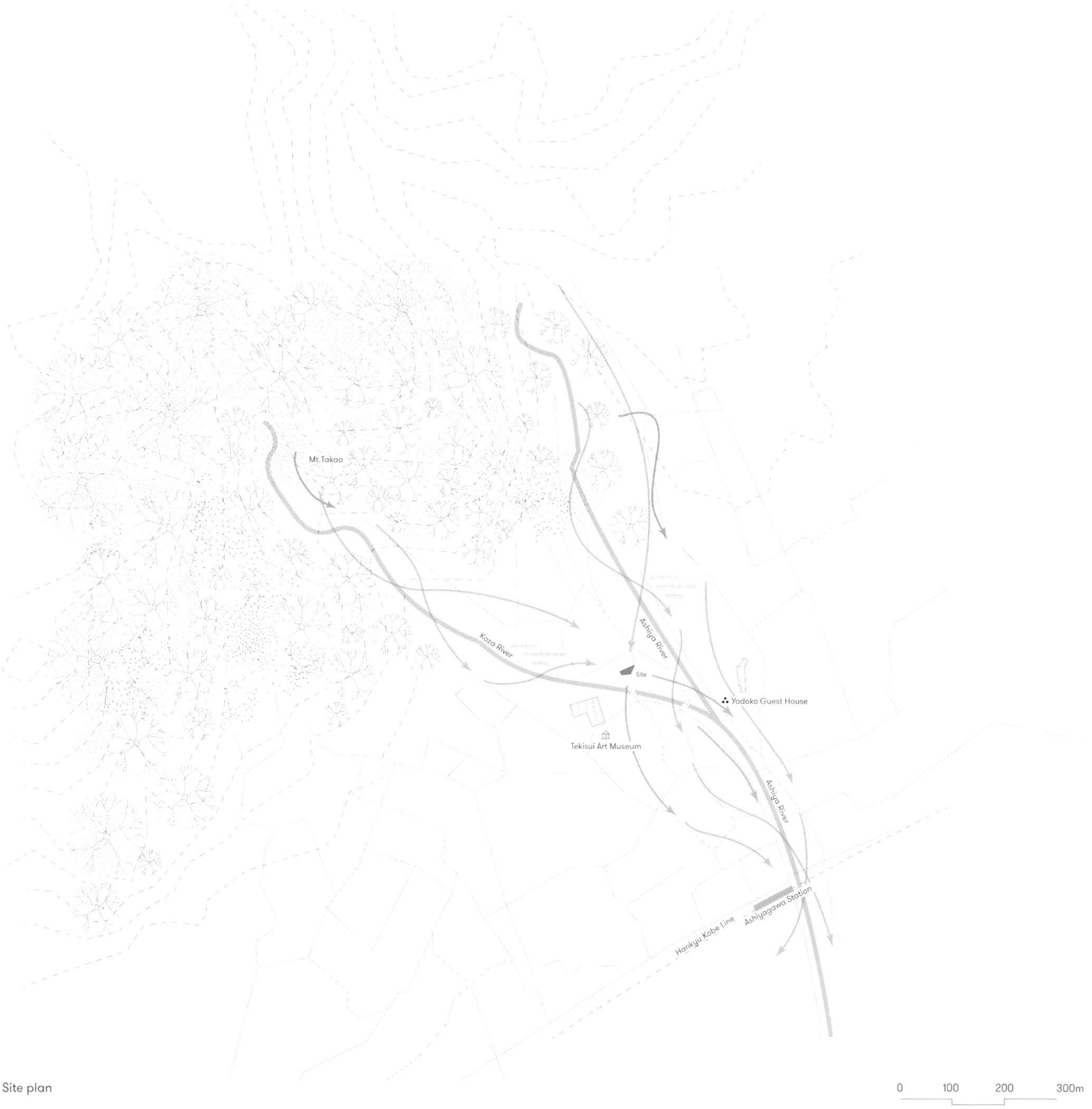

Site plan

Kids' room — the kids' room enjoys the same inter-space relationship as the bedroom

Bathroom — with windows and louverd doors opened, it becomes a semi-outdoor area

Living/dining — looking toward the south, with the windows and louvered doors open

Kitchen/dining — view from the kitchen looking toward the dining area

Living/dining — looking toward the kitchen, with the louvered doors closed

1. Lounge
2. Void
3. Living area
4. Dining
5. Kitchen
6. Bathroom
7. Toilet
8. Entrance
9. Bedroom
10. Main bedroom
11. Walk-in closet
12. Storage

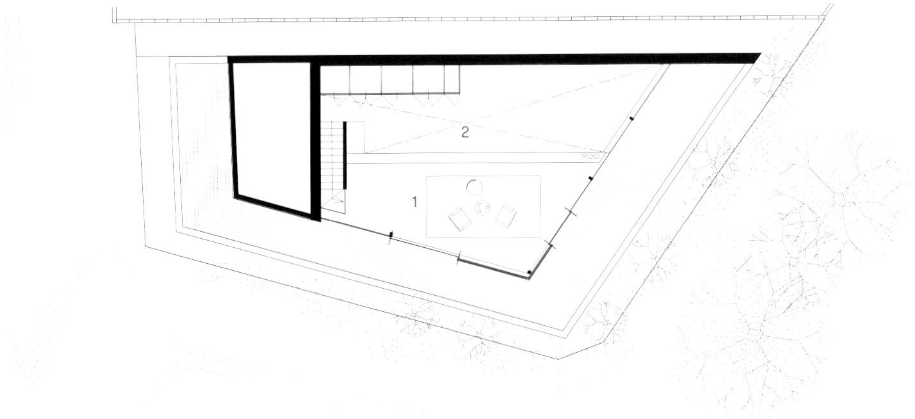

Lounge-floor plan

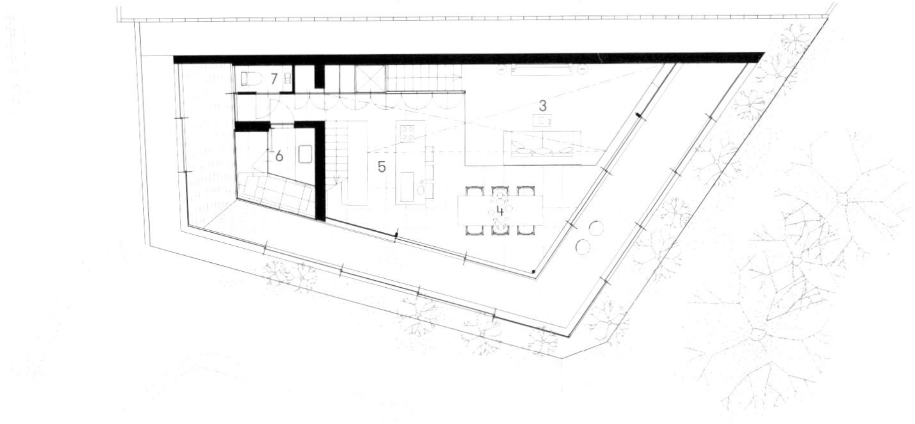

Second-floor plan

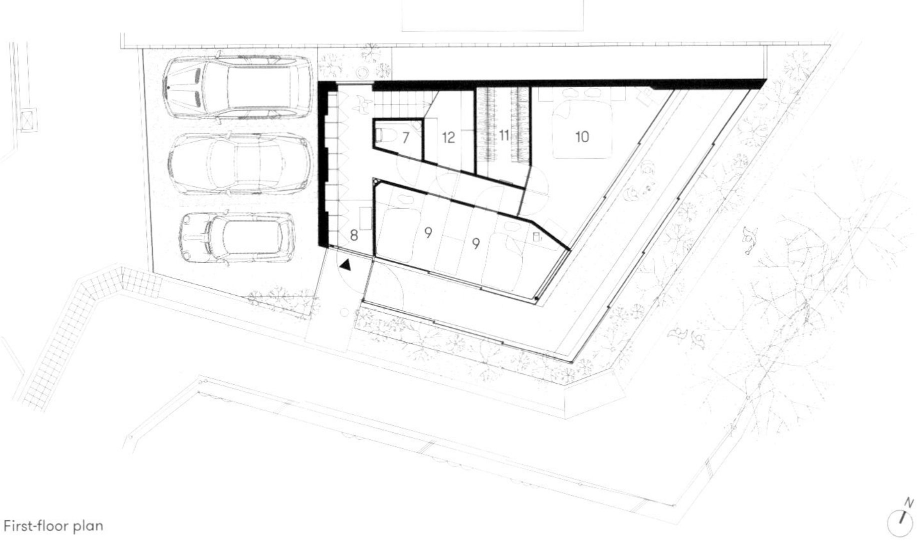

First-floor plan

South elevation

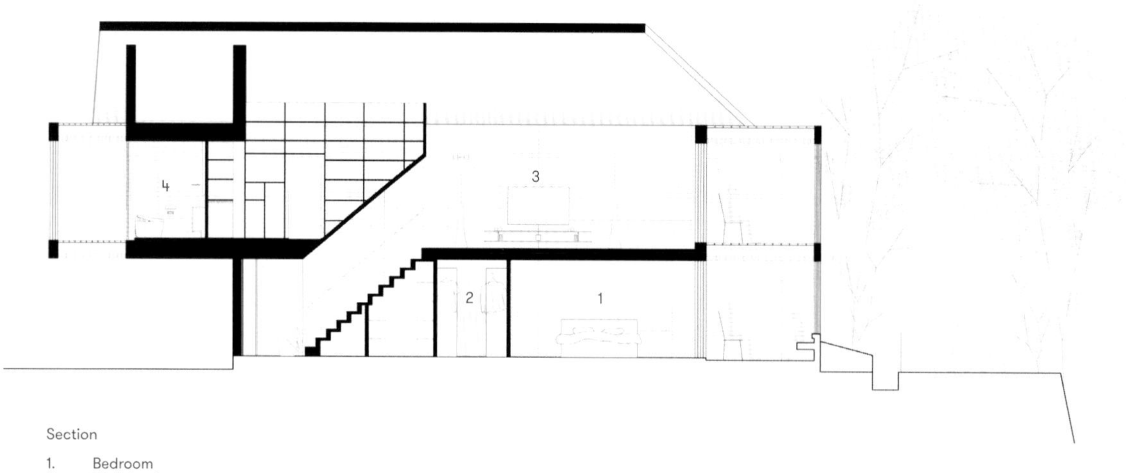

Section

1. Bedroom
2. Walk-in closet
3. Living area
4. Toilet

Living/dining — with all windows and doors opened, the terrace becomes part of the living room

Lounge — view of the lounge; Lloyd Wright's Yamamura House is hidden behind the trees

Mausam – The House of the Season

The monsoon — front view from the main road

Architect firm: Zero Studio, India
Principal architect: Hafeef P. K., Hamid M. M.
Design team: Hafeef P. K., Hamid M. M., Shabna K., Aasish J., Nithin Raj K. J., Kadeeja RASHA, Shafeeq AHMAD
Location: Mannarkad, India
Area: 150 square meters
Completion date: 2017
Photography: Hamid M. M.

Rather than be regarded as a low budget construction, this house would be more aptly perceived as the outcome of a realization that architecture need not be expensive, nor brand new. In developing countries like India, there is a common notion that certain types of architecture represent the financial status of the user, especially where residences are concerned. Like elsewhere in India, this has caused residential architecture in Kerala, too, to drift slowly away from using vernacular materials and techniques, thus compromising climatic responsiveness and energy efficiency. On top of that, the taste of the people these days is also influenced by the prevailing architecture type in the Middle East and Europe, where a majority of Keralites work. Irrespective of the style used, the affluent class has the privilege to afford air-conditioning and automated systems, but the rest who live in the cheaper, at times smaller-scale, replicas don't. They are "condemned" to complain about the lack of comfort inside their "dream-come-true" homes, even after having spent a lion's share of their savings on them.

The attempt here was to create awareness on the importance of having buildings that are true to themselves. The point is: whatever the social status of the owner, residential architecture should speak the language of simplicity and be congruent with the given context of the site, climate, vernacular materials, and their end-user.

The house is placed subtly over a sloping landscape in a rubber plantation, in a setting where it is surrounded by residences that fall into the stereotypes mentioned earlier. As part of a deliberate effort to create a dialog between the building and passers-by, the house has been placed closer to the road. Though rural in setting, considerable traffic passes along the road in the front, which connects several adjoining villages, offering a significant amount of visibility for the building. The interesting part was in having to decide how to make use of this visibility, along with other primary concerns. To go with a modest, simple-looking home in the midst of an array of "expensive-looking" mansions was a crucial point in the whole process, and the rest just followed. This was done without compromising the requirements of the client for a simply built home (not really an indication of his financial status).

The client, a retired army officer, wanted a simple and peaceful home for his family in his ancestral land, and it also had to be a house for two sets of people—him and his wife, and as a house for the whole family.

The inside spaces are placed on three levels connected by stairs. The spaces are designed with dynamic requirements in mind. Hence, the common spaces are expandable and the rest are kept at optimum size. The functional elements actively contribute to the aesthetics of the house; for example, the windows are replaced with brick *jalis* (a perforated brick "screen"). The choice of material has been selected from vernacular options: laterite bricks for the walls, terra cotta tiles for roofing and flooring, natural timber, and so on, and has been brought into the design using local workmanship. Plastering the laterite walls was more affordable, compared with leaving them exposed—exposed walls involve expensive technical expertise, not to mention the installation and required maintenance after.

The interior of the residence is kept minimal, with the structural elements purposefully left bare, keeping the home true to its self. Furniture from the client's old home has also been remodeled and reused. Adding to that, roofing tiles were taken from a demolished house nearby. The clay roofing at varying heights keeps the heat gain from affecting the interiors. Along with the roof and the terra cotta flooring, the ample air movement ensured through the jalis adds to the thermal comfort of the house. The jalis also welcome the play of natural light in the interiors at various times of the day.

The optimization of the design, methodology, and material selection, without compromising the aesthetic appeal of the home, was the key factor in challenging the notion that everything that is affordable must be unattractive. The design of this home is an attempt at proving that affordability is a design style that brings out the best of the elements in a smart way.

The choice of landscape elements was derived from the site and its natural setting, comprising locally grown plants, trees, and the existing rubber plantation. Thus, the visual imagery of the house is transformed with the changing seasons. The house will look dry from the outside during the summer, but inside, things are kept cool. It celebrates the rain during the monsoon, blooms with the spring, and romances with the morning breezes in the winter.

Sit-out and main door — view from the main road

The mud wall — view from the side yard

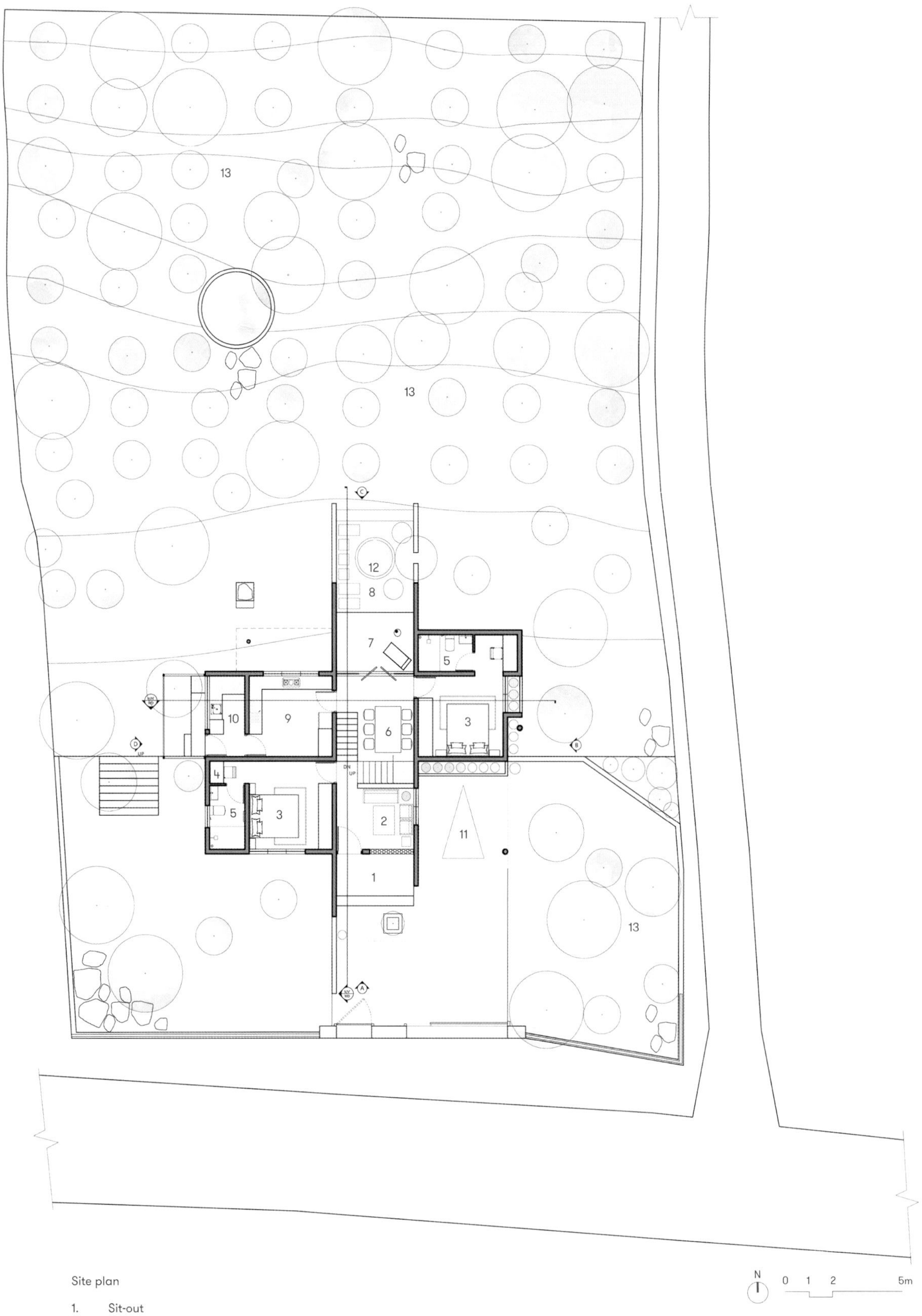

Site plan

1. Sit-out
2. Living room
3. Bedroom
4. Dressing area
5. Bathroom and toilet
6. Dining area
7. Patio
8. Courtyard
9. Kitchen
10. Work area
11. Porch
12. Koi pond
13. Rubber plantation

The entry — view of the split-levels from the main door

Staircase — view toward dining room and patio

Rear garden and koi pond — view toward dining room

Main bedroom

Rear side view

Rear side view — view from the woods

1. Sit-out
2. Living room
3. Bedroom
4. Dressing area
5. Bathroom and toilet
6. Dining area
7. Patio
8. Courtyard
9. Kitchen
10. Work area
11. Balcony
12. Family living area
13. Porch
14. Koi pond

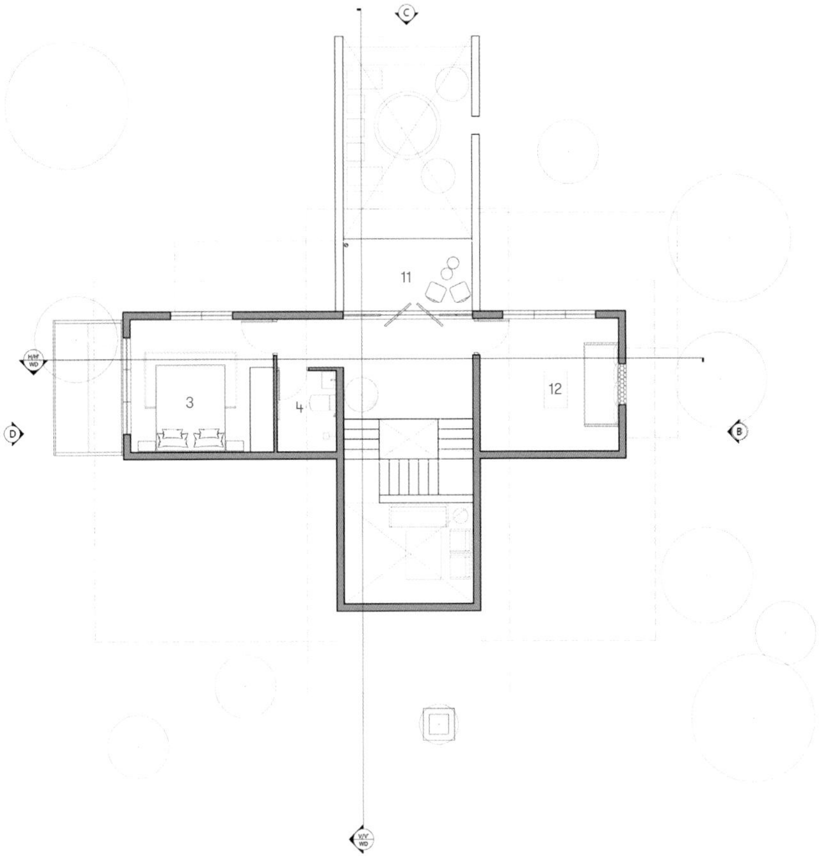

First-floor plan

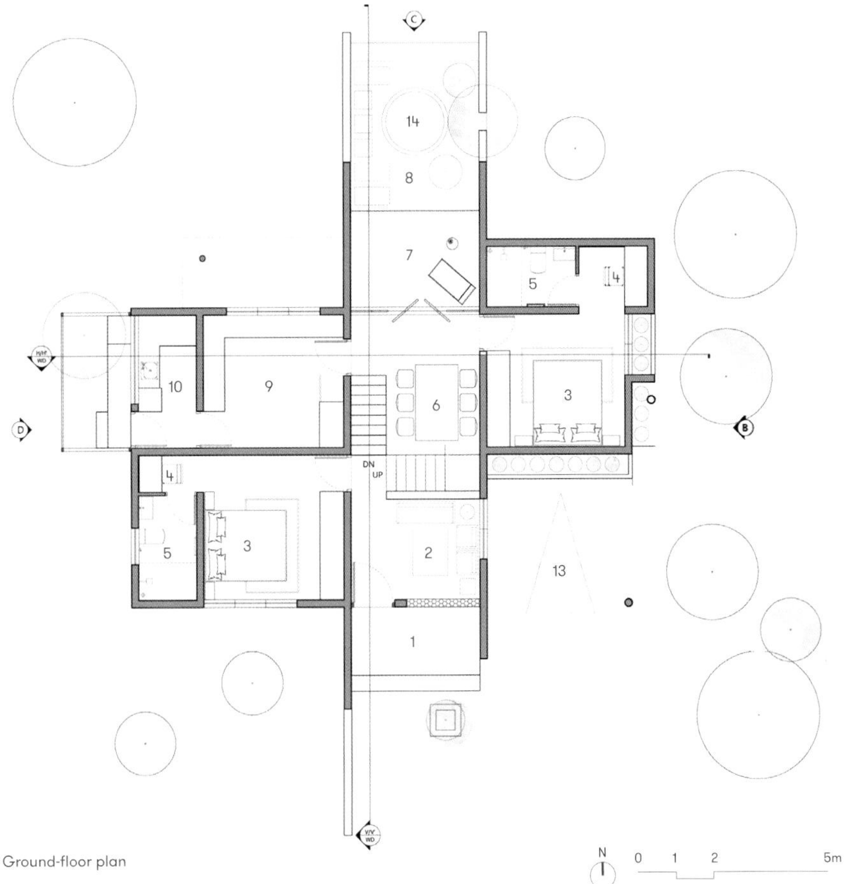

Ground-floor plan

Front view — the rain enhances the rustic scene

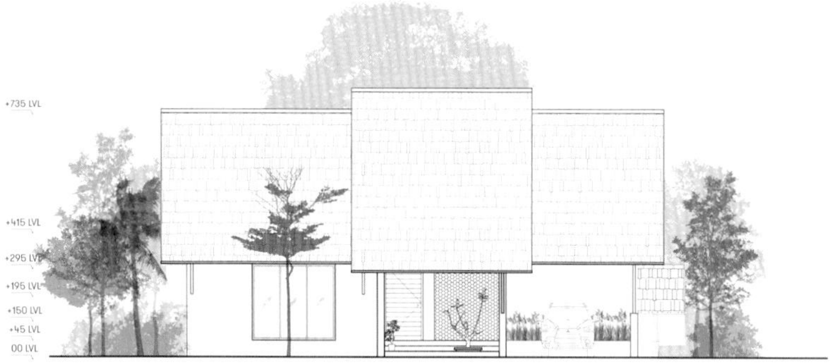

Elevation A

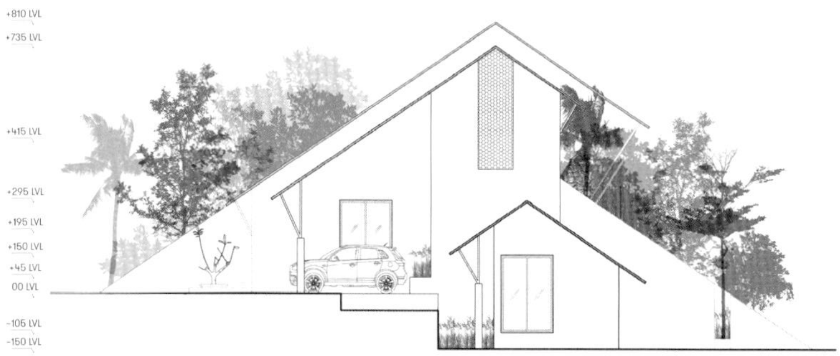

Elevation B

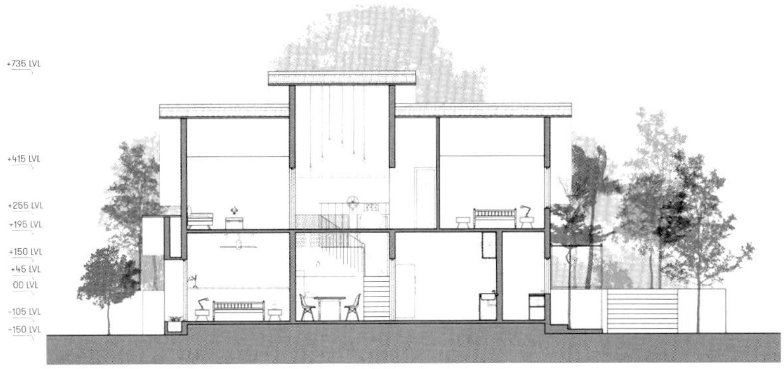

Section HH

Section H'H'

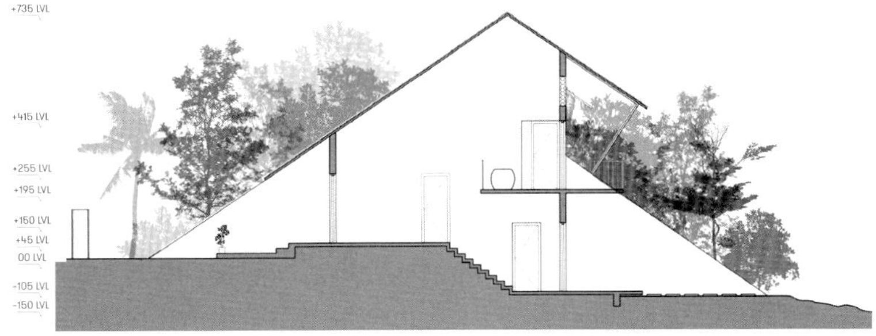

Section VV

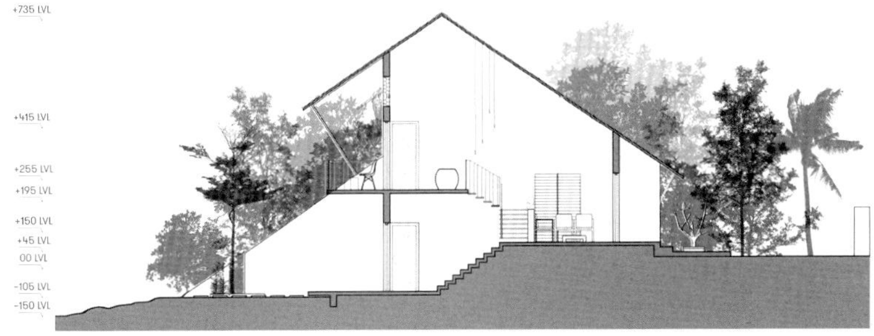

Section V'V'

Chattogram International Trade Fair (CITF) 2020: Collected Memory of the City Dwellers

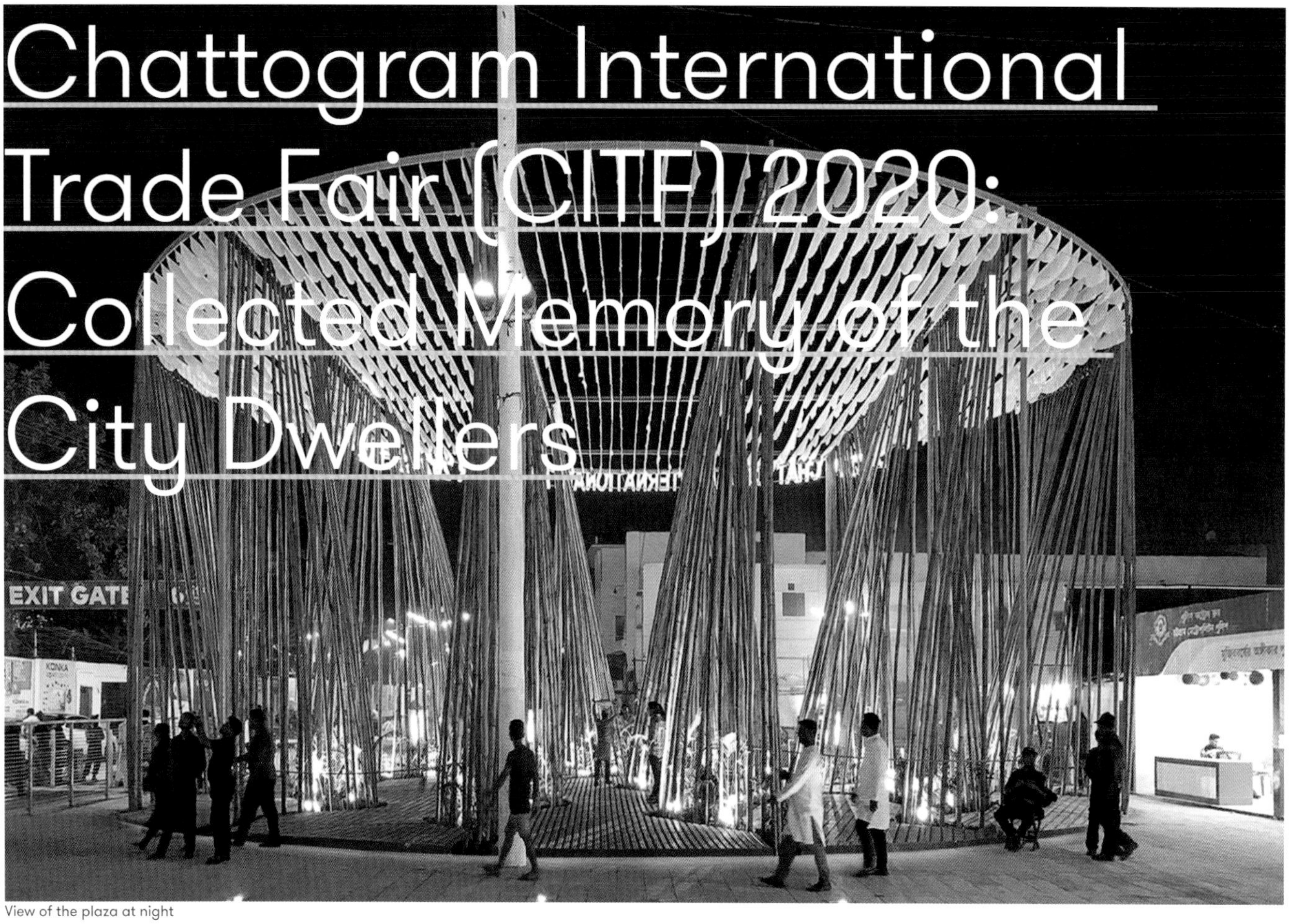

View of the plaza at night

Architect firm: Imran Hasan & team, Bangladesh
Principal architect: Imran HASAN
Design team: Sadia SHARMIN, Arpan SHIL, Sadiqul Islam SHEHAB, Amit Kushum CHOWDHURY, Saad SIDDIQUE
Location: Chattogram, Bangladesh
Site area: 32,000 square meters
Completion date: March 2020
Photography: Imran Hasan & team

Temporary architecture has been increasingly used in urban spaces for transient events and situations. These structures have extended the opportunities for architects to test their understanding of urban spaces and human behavior by challenging the boundaries of architecture. With the master plan of the Chattogram International Trade Fair (CITF) 2020, the architects have tried to explore possibilities for integrating contextual analysis into the design and re-evaluating the idea of a trade fair to craft an experiential environment for the visitors.

CITF has been an annual event in Chattogram city for the last twenty-seven years. It is the second-largest trade fair in Bangladesh, with an estimated two million visitors annually. In contrast to the short construction period (approximately thirty days), the design and organization phase took several months. The event ran for forty days.

The design begin by collecting stories of city dwellers through a podcast titled *Chattogram Echoes*, where they shared fond memories of an earlier, "greener" time. Most of the narrations conveyed a nostalgia for a green landscape, open spaces, and less traffic in the city. However, rapid urbanization has left hardly any of those memories or places intact. These conversations guided the team to consider how placemaking is negotiated, focusing on people's experiences in urban spaces.

In the previous years' CITF layouts, all the major access points and circulation paths were dominated by vehicular movements, prioritizing construction work and the daily supply of products. This time around, the vehicular thoroughfare in the master plan was altered, allowing the design to introduce a 90-by-15-meter plaza dedicated to the visitors. Under a fabric canopy, the plaza accommodated sitting areas, a fountain, floor lights, and plants.

To design the main entrance, the architects reconceptualized the idea of the gate, so that it went from being a doorway to a spatial experience; a circular bamboo installation (20 meters in diameter and 10 meters in height) was designed. This acted as a transitional space to lead the visitors into the plaza. All the materials were locally sourced and reused after demolition.

The master plan included twenty pavilions, 200 stalls, three international zones, a food court, a gaming zone, a prayer space, male and female toilet facilities, car parking, a security booth, an admin office, a fire service, a police security booth, and a power supply station. The design process was flexible enough to address the challenges during construction and to collaborate with various professional and local technicians.

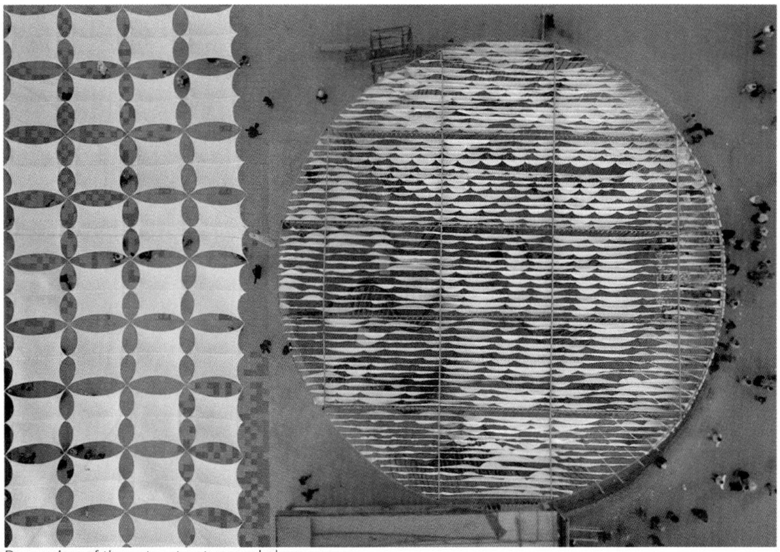

Drone view of the entry structure and plaza canopy

The plaza's canopy creates shadow patterns within the plaza during the day

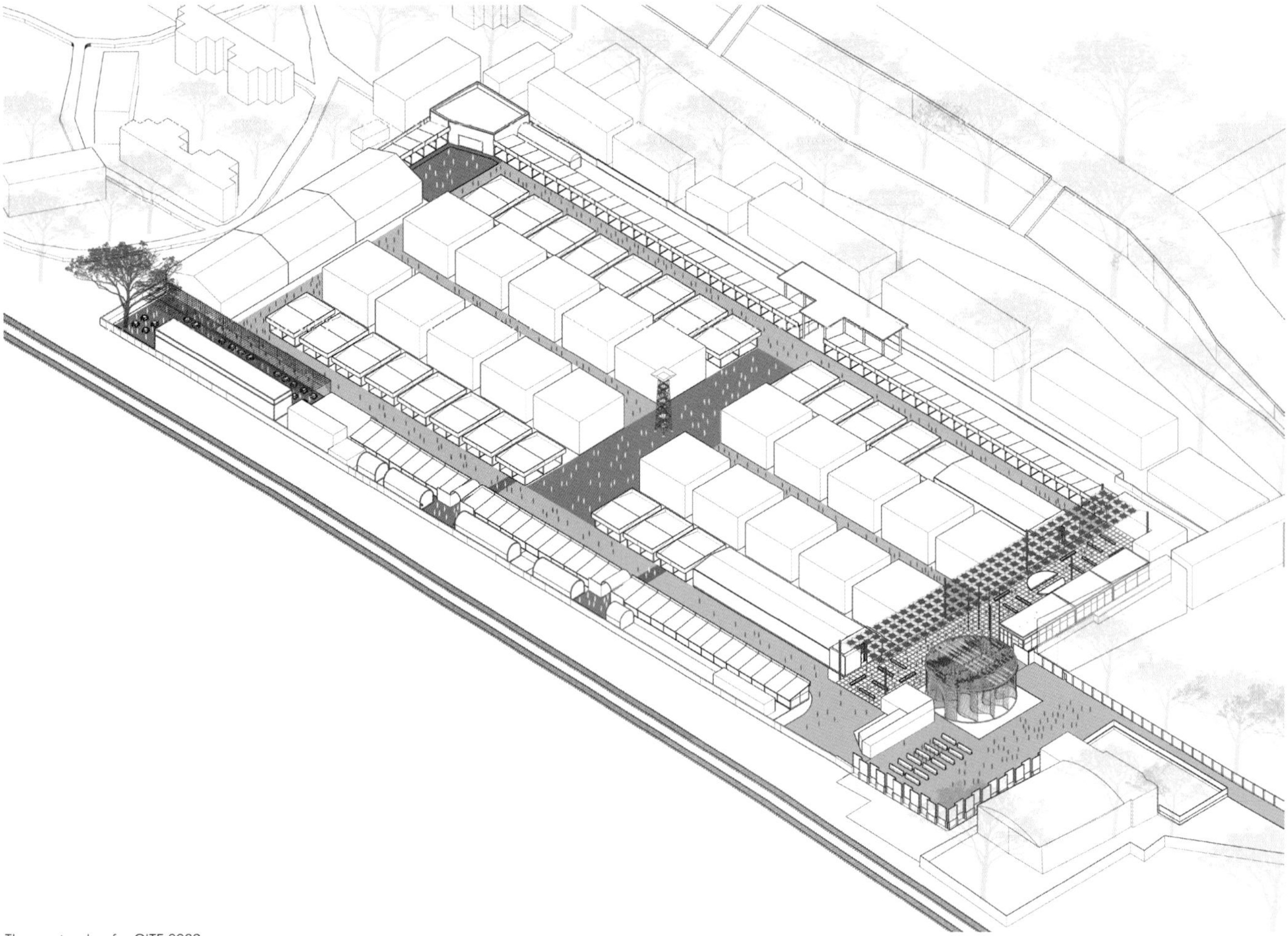
The masterplan for CITF 2020

Activity mapping in the front plaza

The entrance has five separated pathways to handle large crowds

Children playing with floor lights at the plaza

A schoolboy enjoying the walk through the bamboo installation

a. Bamboo was used for the entrance structure to add natural texture to the space
b. Recycled bamboo plywood from a shipbreaking yard was used for the floor platform of the entrance structure
c. All the floor tiles for the event were locally produced and reused after the event
d. Recycled steel pipes were used as structural members
e. All fabric was sourced from the local market (Terry Bazaar), and tailors used their skill to complete the sewing to meet the design
f. The bricks used for the toilet structure were recycled after the fair was dismantled

Façade detail

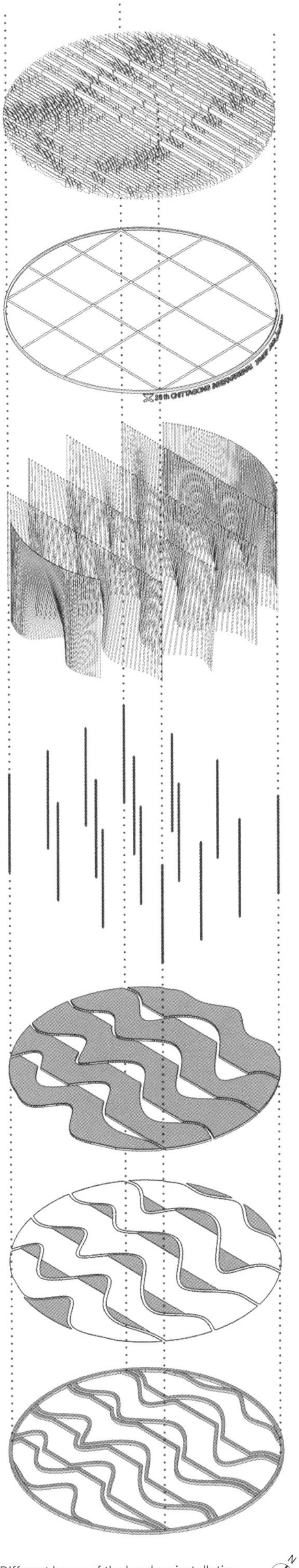

Different layers of the bamboo installation

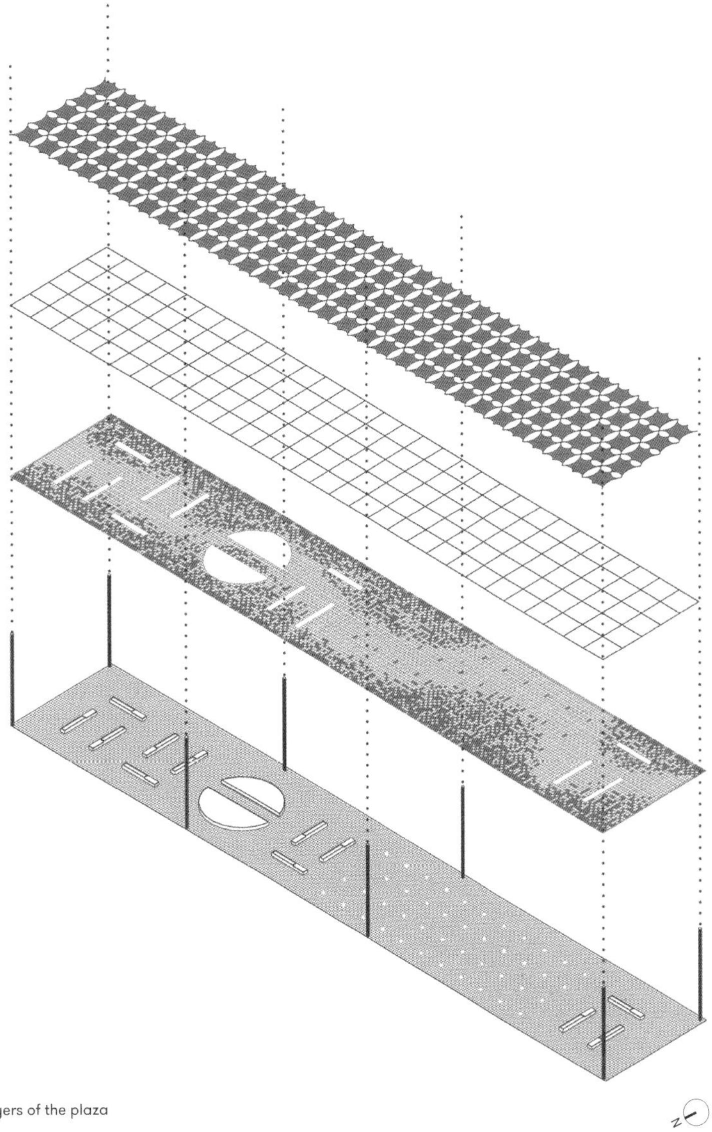

Different layers of the plaza

The plants, bamboo, and "flowing" fabrics on the roof create a cheerful environment as one enters the fair

The layers of fabric over the entry structure create a rippling effect in the wind

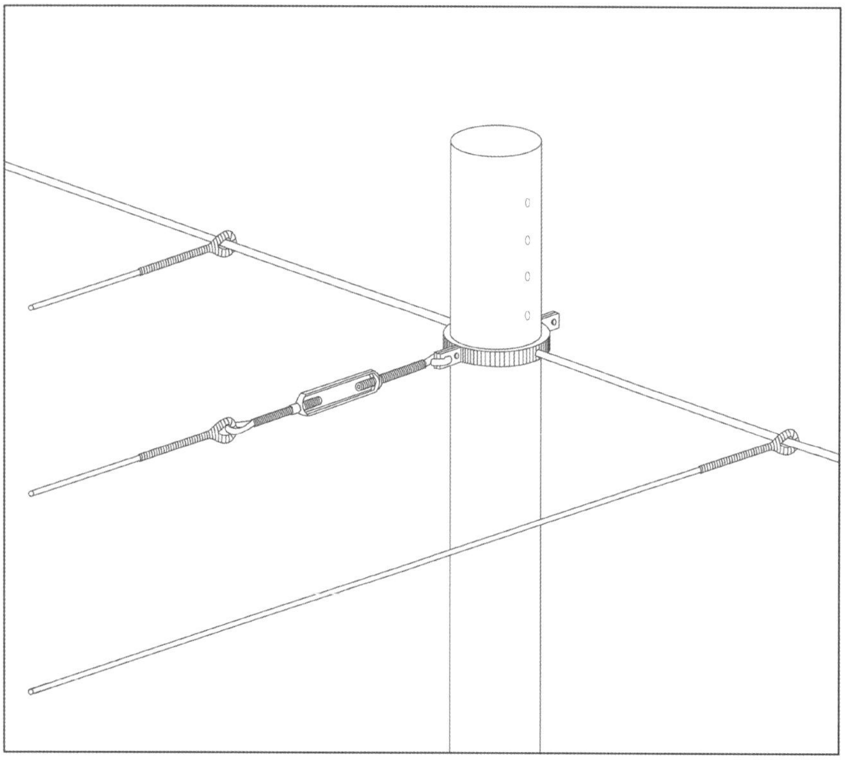

Construction details

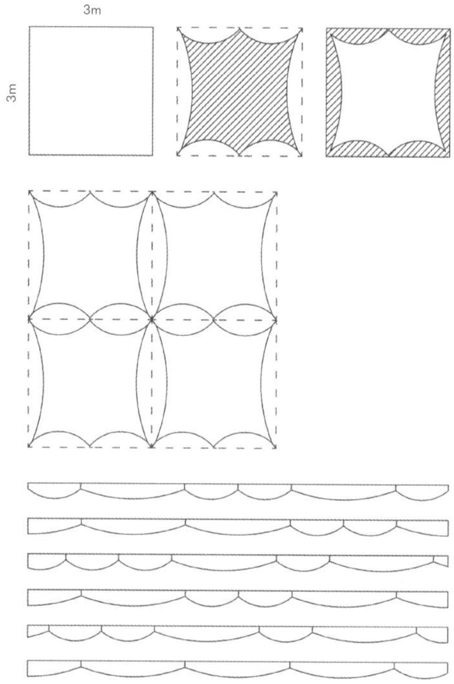

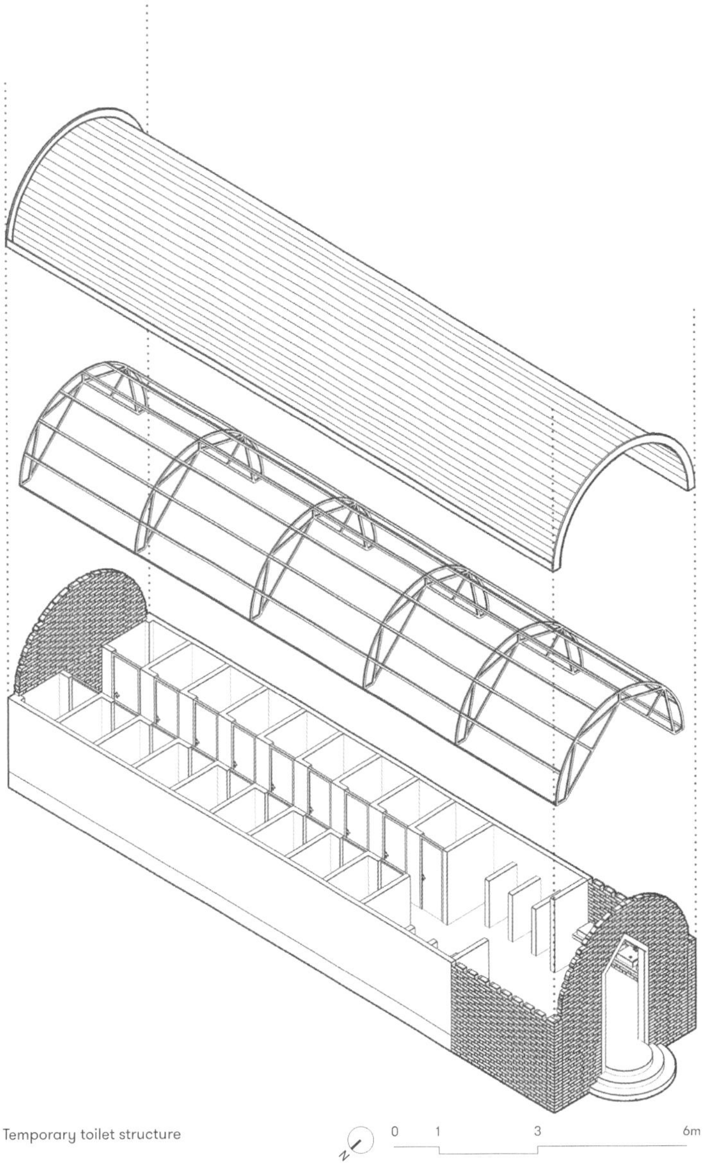

Temporary toilet structure

Temporary toilet structure

Integral

Southern view of the spinning factory and the central lake

Architect firm: Ronald Lu & Partners, Hong Kong, China
Principal architect: Guymo WONG
Design team: Henry CHEUNG, Matthias MA, Darren TSANG, ZHU Mufeng, Tim WILLIAMS
Location: Guilin, China
Area: 285,725 square meters
Completion date: September 2020
Photography: Arch-Exist, WU Qingshan

Integral is a sustainable and state-of-the-art spinning and garment manufacturing plant. Located near scenic Guilin in China's Guangxi Province, Integral is situated in a wetland area that was once the site of a brick factory. Damaged by the brick manufacturing activities, the original wetland was in poor shape. The architects sought to rehabilitate the land and turn a spoiled former manufacturing area into a new type of conservation-led development.

In the past, textile and garment manufacturing was regarded as a traditional, low-tech processing industry, characterized by stark, functional factory buildings and emissions of pollution. Integral's design is a world away from this old perception. It is a place where people, technology, and the natural environment can exist in harmony. While manufacturing is still the focus of Integral, the project also includes a botanical garden with natural dye crops, as well as a wetland and eco-tourism functions, such as an experience and learning center that showcases how traditional labor-intensive manufacturing has been transformed by technology into a technologically advanced process that respects workers and embraces local culture.

The design of Integral began by studying the site's topography and geology. The history and culture of Guilin were also respected, as were the area's unique landscape features and contexts—reflection, layering, colors, and textures. All these elements are tactfully revealed in the building's massing and envelope design. The design team then began restoring the original wetland landscape. Even before ground was broken, this over-exploited site was intentionally left alone for a year to allow nature to slowly restore itself. Only when new plant life finally sprouted and flocks of egrets arrived, the true beginning of the project was realized.

The guiding design principle was to retain as much of the site's ecology as possible, including the bamboo groves, fish ponds, and wetlands to the north of the site. The team placed the larger building blocks on the expansive dry area at the site's south side, a place that had been degraded by the old factory's excavation activities. The largest excavated pit that was "left over" was restored to a natural waterbody, with a few staff dining facilities situated along the lakeshore, that are designed to echo the design of the buildings to the south, yet remain in harmony with the lake.

The highest point of Integral is only 22 meters in elevation. The design intentionally extends the main building horizontally instead of vertically, seamlessly integrating the large production workshop and craft center with the natural environment. In turn, this makes the site's greenery the main focus, with the buildings playing a supporting role in the overall aesthetic. Elements of the local architectural language and culture appear everywhere, with distinctive blue bricks and bamboo panels used extensively in the buildings' exteriors including a large, semi-transparent bamboo curtain placed on the façade of the large craft center's wall to soften and break up the building's massing.

A large percentage of the craft center's roof is also covered with green plants, which increase the overall greenery coverage and also help to insulate the building to keep indoor temperatures stable. Some of these plants belong to the rooftop farm, which will—in keeping with the project's sustainable values—provide fresh organic produce for the staff restaurant.

At its heart, Integral is a human-centered project that has the utmost respect for nature. Integral reimagines how architecture, manufacturing, and the natural world can coexist, providing a pioneering model of how businesses can create a balance between nature and humanity, while simultaneously ensuring the industrial advancement of society.

A bird's-eye view of Integral from the west of the site

The southern façade of the garment factory allows ample daylight into the factory interior

East side view of the garment factory and warehouse, with the dining hall in the background

Nature, manufacturing, and humanity coexist in harmony

The greenery and outdoor team-building area surrounded by spinning and garment factories

The staff can connect with nature during their journey to work

Food crops and greenery growing on the factory rooftop

1. Parking
2. Native fauna/flora Island
3. Main entrance
4. Khun Opera
5. Pier 4
6. Pier 2
7. Lake
8. Pond
9. Pier 5
10. Plant filtration demonstration
11. Pier 1
12. Multipurpose area
13. Staff entrance
14. VIP dining
15. Bamboo forest
16. Loading bay
17. Visitor center
18. Outdoor exhibition
19. Osmanthus forest
20. Liriore field

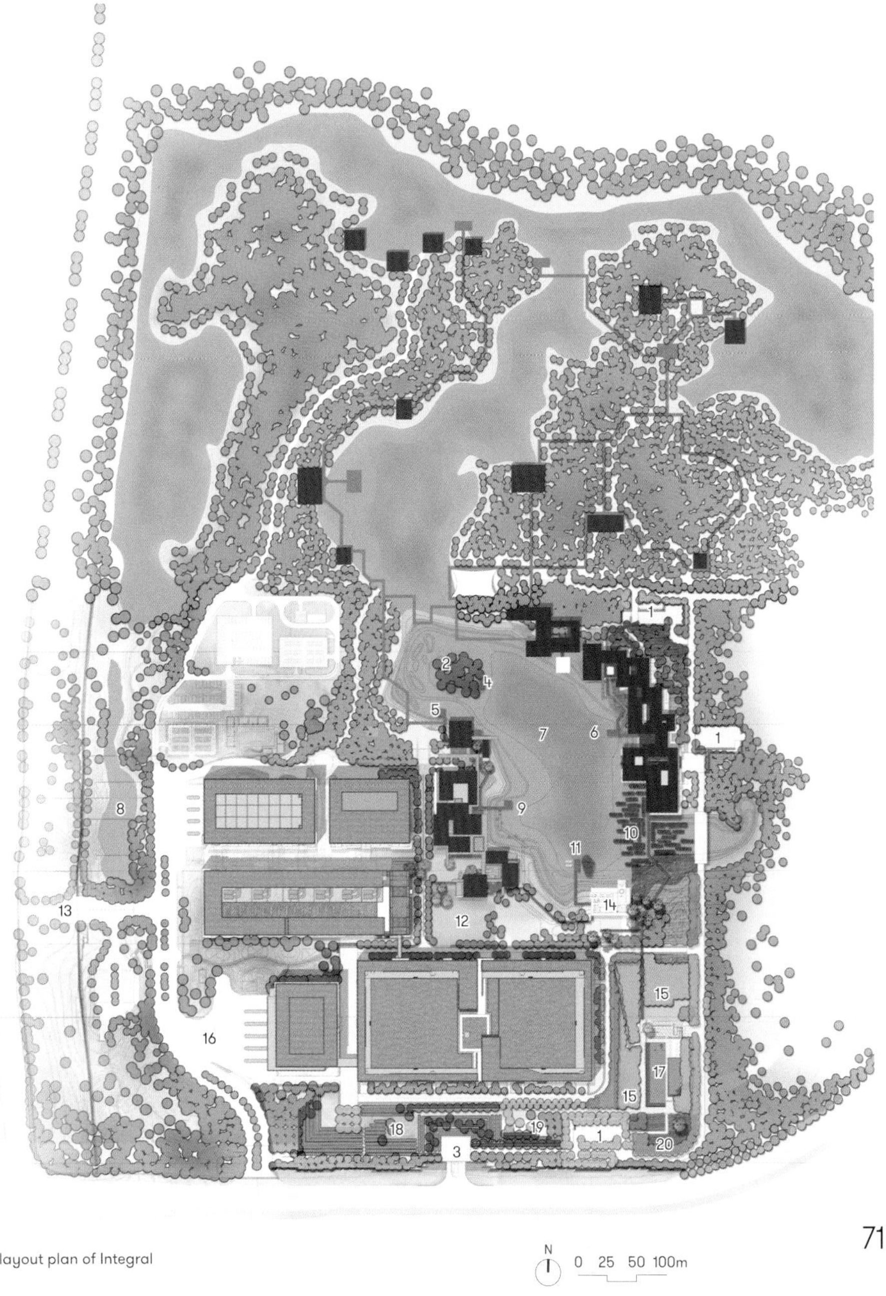

Master layout plan of Integral

Staff can dine at a noodle bar or take a rest in the garden

View from inside the garment factory looking out into the garden

The bamboo façade creates a transitional space between solid structure and nature

Interplay of light and shadow seen along the visitors' route

View of the semi-transparent bamboo graded curtain on the façade

Noor

Approach to the building

Architect firm: DWm4 Architects, Bangladesh
Principal architect: Mahmudul Anwar RIYAAD, Mamnoon Murshed CHOWDHURY
Design team: Mahmudul Anwar RIYAAD, Mamnoon Murshed CHOWDHURY, Muhammad Farhad HOSSAIN, Sabiha Sultana SARA, Obidur RAHMAN
Location: Nabiganj, Bangladesh
Area: 530 square meters
Completion date: November 2018
Photography: Maruf RAIHAN

Noor was designed with an aim to reconstruct memories—the memories of a family of six children and a septuagenarian mother who had occasionally lived on the property four decades ago. Today, the ancestral property is subdivided among heirs and the family's inherited share sits at the farthest point, accessible only through a 2-meter-wide alley. The other families had already built on their plots without leaving much open space and this had created a dense series of buildings.

Nostalgia and a fondness of their younger days spurred the two brothers, Mamoon and Junaid, to build a house on their rather oddly shaped 285-square-meter property, where their family could reconnect to the memories of a time when their father had been alive. But how will architecture recreate memory? This was the challenge in an otherwise functionally simple residential project located on the fringes of Narayanganj, a city in central Bangladesh.

The house, therefore, was not conceived as a composition of three-dimensional forms that is complete, but rather as a container of a sequence of experiences that negotiates with its surroundings in terms of form, space, and enclosure.

The zoning of spaces was derived from the anticipated lifestyles of the inhabitants during their stay. Almost every other week, the mother comes over from Dhaka to stay for a few days and spend time with members of the greater family from the neighboring houses, as well as old acquaintances. Her room is situated at the ground level, with an adjacent space for casual meetings or gatherings. As visitors, too, often stay for lunch or dinner, the dining room, is set within the closest proximity.

When the brothers are visiting, people from the locality come over, often in groups, to meet them. In such times, the mother would require her privacy. Therefore, the living room is set apart by inserting it into the entry court and the stairs. The screened entry court also ensures visual privacy from the adjacent buildings, while bringing in light and air. The face of this double-height space is a wall with perforations—its geometry is reminiscent of the ornamental pattern of a handwoven cotton saree. This wall is like the cover page of the house, the giver of light and air, the center

The home, Noor, and its context

View toward the front court

that holds the spaces together—it is the tribute to the family's matriarch.

During the design development phase, a 135-square-meter piece of land was added on the southeast side as a precious outdoor living area, intended not only for use by the residents of the house, but also by neighboring relatives. The lawn became the centerpiece for the cluster of all five houses. Another small portion of land was bought and added later during construction, where a small pavilion was constructed as a counterpoint at the end of the lawn. This semi-outdoor space, meant for casual meetings of neighbors and visitors from adjacent villages, is complete with restroom facilities and an ablution space. In the final layout, the lawn, thereby, becomes a hub for the surrounding built forms.

Strips of lands were sacrificed on both sides to widen both the internal path and the external road on the east, in the process making a contribution (of sorts) to the neighborhood. In terms of form, the two-storied lower volume on the lawn is connected with the three-storied volume through the lightwell and staircase. The lightwell—which is also the formal entry, with its perforated wall, waterbody, and small wooden bridge—is the hub of the house itself and is designed to be a spatial multitasker. It was an important consideration in the design that the mass should not overpower the neighbors' houses in scale; it works as an aesthetic infill of humble nature.

In the attempt to recreate memories, elements from the family's old house are reused. These include furniture, electric switches, and ceiling fans. The load-bearing wall structure, wooden shutters, vertical safety grills, whitewashed unadorned plastered walls, green kota stone floor, and terra-cotta-tiled roof terraces are all a part of a conscious scheme to make the family feel at home in the company of elements from a cherished past.

The house is symbolically named "Noor," meaning "light," in honor of Mrs. Noorjahan Begum and Mr. Nooruddin—the parents of the six children.

The connecting bridge beside the stairs

A cozy corner overlooking the entry court

Window at the entry court

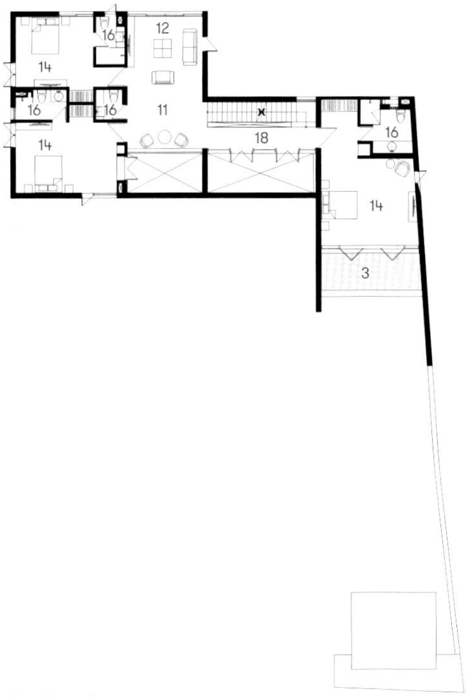

First-floor plan

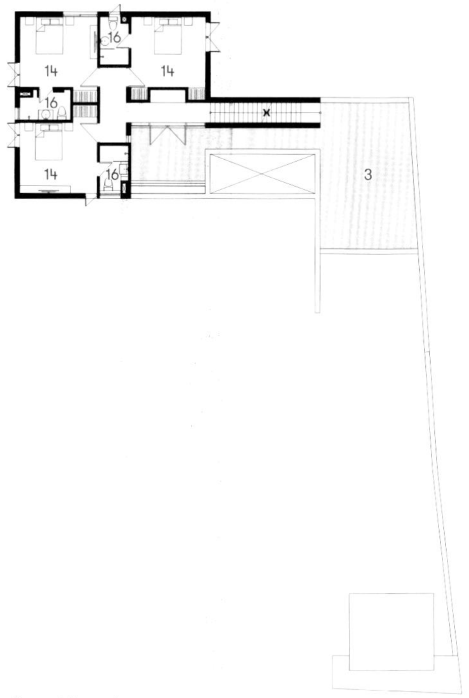

Second-floor plan

1. Pavilion
2. Lawn
3. Terrace
4. Waterbody
5. Entry gate
6. Ablution area
7. Pantry
8. Store
9. Living area
10. Foyer
11. Lobby
12. Family living room
13. Dining
14. Bedroom
15. Kitchen
16. Bathroom and toilet
17. Electrical & pump room
18. Bridge
19 Deck

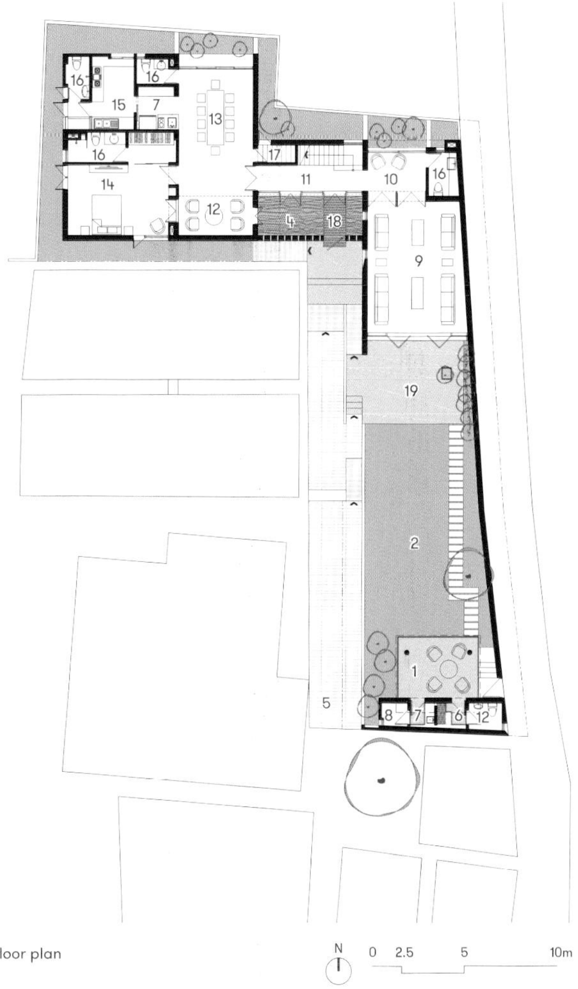

Ground-floor plan

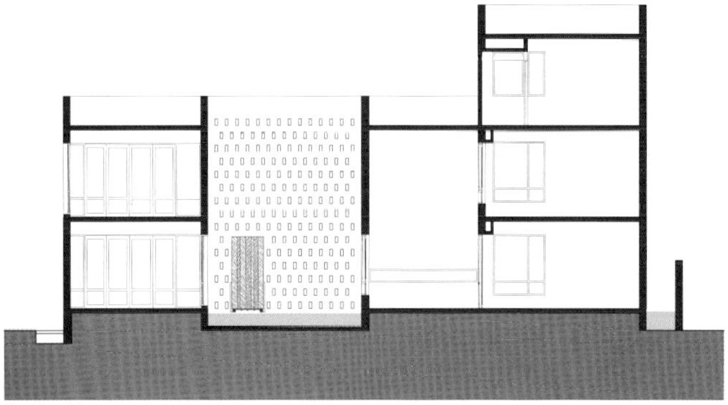

Section AA

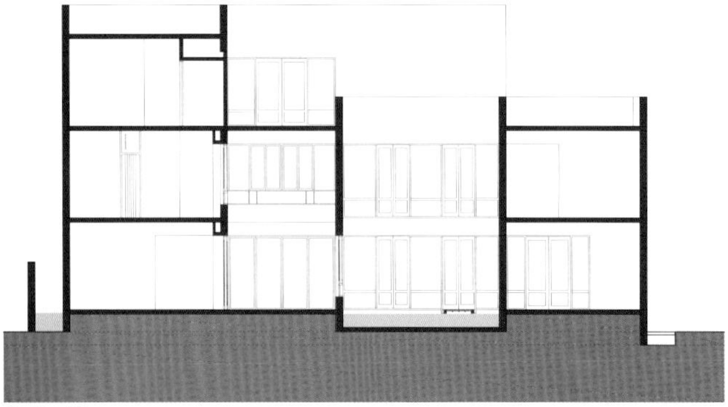

Section BB

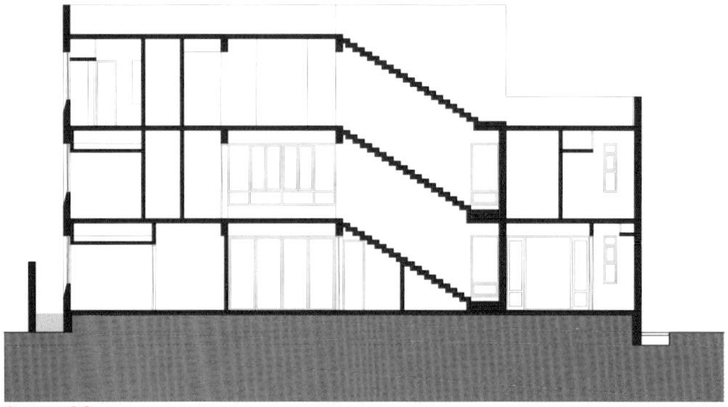

Section CC

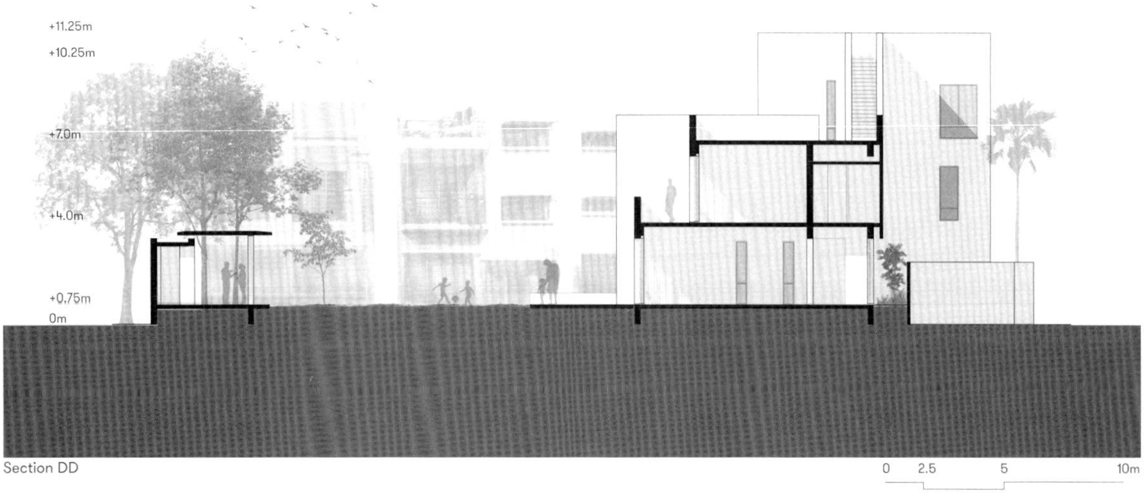

Section DD

Stairs leading to roof

On the way to the terra-cotta terrace

Screen wall

House ATO

Settling in the city © TIAN Fangfang

Architect firm: Atelier Deshaus, China
Principal architect: LIU Yichun
Design team: SHEN Wen, DENG Rui, GONG Yu
Location: Beijing, China
Area: 160 square meters
Completion date: April 2018
Photography: WU Qingshan, TIAN Fangfang

As a result of the housing shortages before the 1980s, living spaces in China were mostly collective. Kitchens often lined up along the halls and public bathrooms, and bottles of laundry detergent became the rudiments of shared space. Despite their unsatisfying spatial conditions, however, Chinese families of that time still enjoyed colorful, neighborly relationships. In housing constructions after the 80s, communal space was minimized so as to obtain as much private space as possible. The living patterns within apartments, where one elevator leads to two households on each floor, resulted in seclusion among neighbors, and sometimes alienation. With the rising popularity of social media networks in recent years, interpersonal interactions have become an indispensable part of the daily lives of the new generation and relationships among people are being redefined.

Dwelling has long since become part of the human body. If one thinks about it, one may discover that the deeper structure of human construction has remained unchanged. From the original primitive hut of Marc-Antoine Laugier, to Chinese wooden architecture—which has been inherited over more than four thousand years—and along to modern housing like the Farnsworth House by Ludwig Mies van der Rohe, the elements for construction of a building can always be simplified into the three visual components of the Chinese character "舍" (*she*)—the top "亼" symbolizing the rooftop, the middle "屮" symbolizing the beam/support, and the base "口" symbolizing the foundation/wall. It seems, the history of human construction has far surpassed that of written characters, and the composition of "亼屮口" (roof, beam, foundation) has almost become a root metaphor that transcends different cultures.

The design of House ATO is a minimalist interpretation of these three elements. It is an application of a precise, contemporary structure, with 5-by-5-centimeter slender square pillars and an ultrathin rooftop measuring 5 centimeters in thickness. Technology may have brought changes in form, but not in the fundamental structure of space. The changes in the ways of living, nevertheless, are presented on the surface of the house. Ten interchangeable furniture boxes are pushed to the outermost layer of the living space and become part of the building envelope, which implies the increasing openness of today's modern living space.

The space is divided into three layers from the outside to the inside: open and outward spaces under the eaves, flexible furniture that can be opened or closed, and the most private space for the bathroom. In the daytime, the space under the eaves or the extended furniture space can turn into cafés, ramen restaurants, barbershops or conference rooms, and so on. It returns to being an intimate home at night when all boxes are closed and living components are unfolded. The furniture carries the personalities and life definitions of the residents, and is a communal space in itself as well, just like the collectiveness carried by the character "舍"(*she*): "Settling in the city, means *she*."

Enclosed interchangeable furniture © WU Qingshan

View from the north © WU Qingshan

Interchangeable furniture as a living space © TIAN Fangfang

Northeast elevation © TIAN Fangfang

The skylight © WU Qingshan

Southeast elevation © WU Qingshan

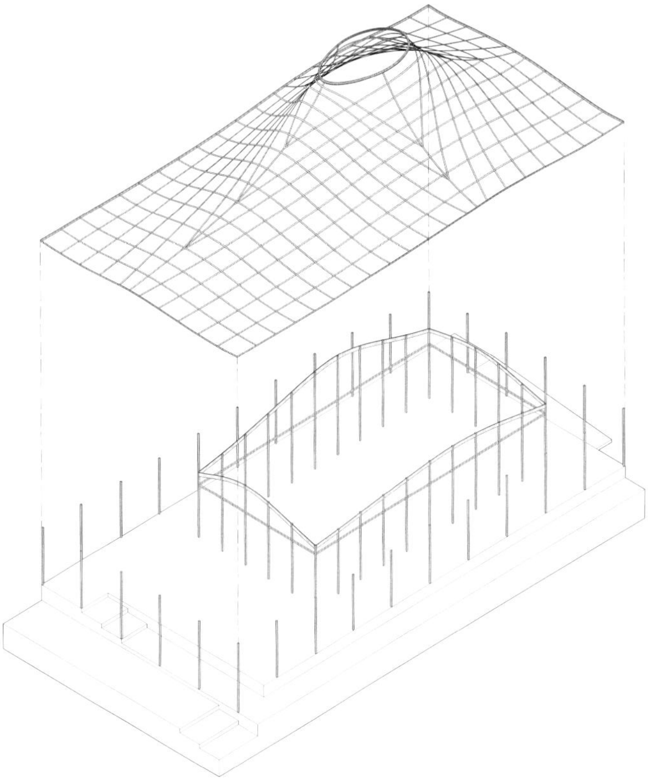

Structural axonometric diagram © Atelier Deshaus

Detail © TIAN Fangfang

Communal space on the porch © TIAN Fangfang

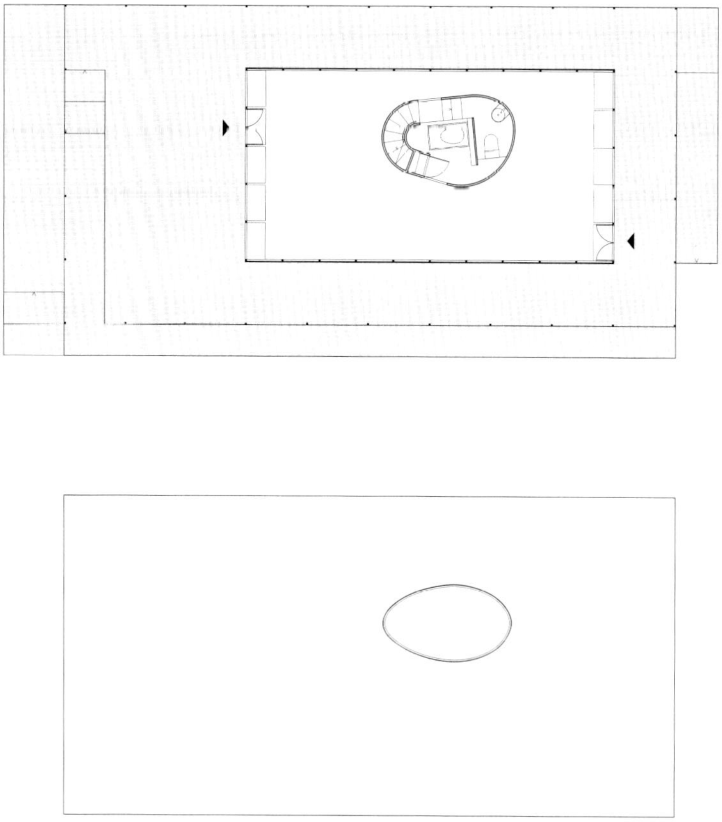

Plans © Atelier Deshaus

0 1 5 10m

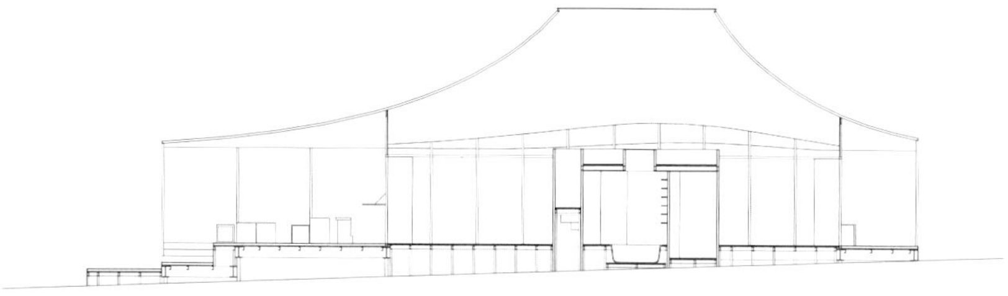

Section 1 © Atelier Deshaus

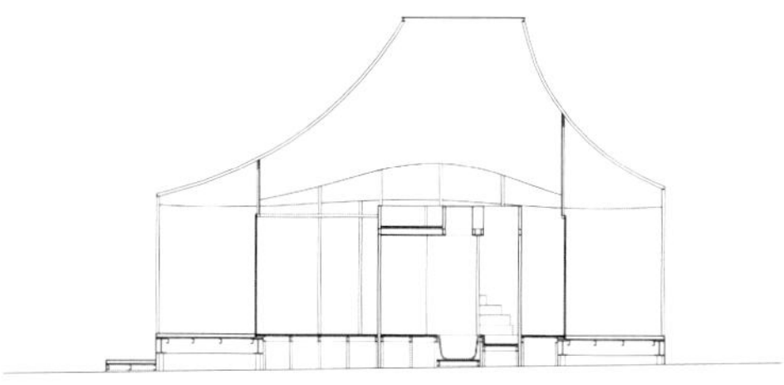

Section 2 © Atelier Deshaus

0 1 5 10m

Xi'an Silk Road International Conference Center

Façade of the main entrance at night

Architect firm: Tongji Architectural Design (Group) Co., Ltd., China; Shanghai Tongji Urban Planning & Design Institute Co., Ltd., China; Architekten von Gerkan, Marg und Partner, Germany
Principal architect: TANG Shuoning, Magdalene WEIß
Design team: QIU Dongqing, YU Xueyue, HU Junfeng, DONG Tianxiang, CHEN Rong
Location: Xi'an, China
Area: 207, 112 square meters
Completion date: March 2020
Photography: SU Shengliang

The Xi'an Silk Road International Conference Center is located in the core area of the Eurasian Economy Zone in the Chanba Ecological Area, west of Huizhan Avenue and south of Xianghuaier Road. Together with the Silk Road International Exhibition Center on the west side, it represents the core project for trade and industrial development in Shaanxi Province. The project remedies the lack of large-scale professional conference centers in Xi'an and the northwest region, continues the historical context, meets the needs of the times, and creates a new landmark for Xi'an along the New Silk Road.

The project has a total construction area of 207,112 square meters and a height of 51.05 meters. The three floors aboveground (partially equipped with a mezzanine) account for 128,369 square meters and the two floors that are partially underground account for 78,743 square meters. The building offers conference spaces, banqueting spaces, and multifunctional facilities. These three main programs stack up in three levels aboveground, situating a banquet hall on the first floor—with a height of 16 meters, a large multifunction hall on the second floor—with a height of 16 meters, and a main conference hall on the third floor—with a height of 18.45 meters.

The design of the façade of the Xi'an Silk Road Conference Center applies an abstract and straightforward strategy for inheriting and translating traditional Chinese architecture. Positioned in front of a high, transparent, concave, retreating, curved, glazed curtain wall, the upper and lower parts of the longitudinally symmetrical crescent-shaped cornices are linked by twenty-four groups of suspended slender steel columns. They form an iconic image that is at once modern and classic, grand and refined, and solemn and elegant.

The overall design attempts to capture the essence of Chinese classical architecture. The conference center as a whole, has a square and symmetrical layout, with landscape water and sunken courtyards arranged symmetrically to each side of the south, east, and west axes. In addition, the 200-meter-long side building volume is also symmetrical and unified, with four façades. The lower crescent-shaped cornices are cantilevered below the suspended column system and the transparent, glazed curtain walls surround the first floor on all sides above the podium. These form a spacious and shadowed entrance space, creating a picture in which the building appears to float. When people reach the main entrance located on the central axis through the bridge above the landscape water, they experience a sequential space full of a sense of ritual. Adding to that, the composition of the ascending square base, the upper and lower crescent-shaped cornices with stretching contours, and the rational and regular columns were also guided by a balanced and harmonious sense of proportion, reflecting the inheritance and contemporary expression of Chinese classical architecture.

The construction of the conference center accommodates a dialog between the purity and the complexity of the building:
· The pure and grand architectural space is in dialog with the complex banqueting and conference functions and circulation systems.
· The pure façade form is in dialog with the complex layout of each floor.
· The pure 200-by-200-meter aboveground column-free structural system is in dialog with the complex seismic load system.
· The refined interior decoration finishes are in dialog with the complex mechanical and electrical supply systems.

Aerial view along the river

Lateral façade

View across water at dusk

Glazed curtain wall on the front façade

Suspended columns

Interior view of the southeast corner

The main entrance's lobby

1. Secondary entrance hall
2. Council chamber
3. VIP entrance hall
4. Lounge
5. VIP room
6. Dining
7. Kitchen
8. Banquet hall
9. Lobby
10. Entrance hall
11. Outdoor terrace
12. Multifunctional hall
13. Main conference hall

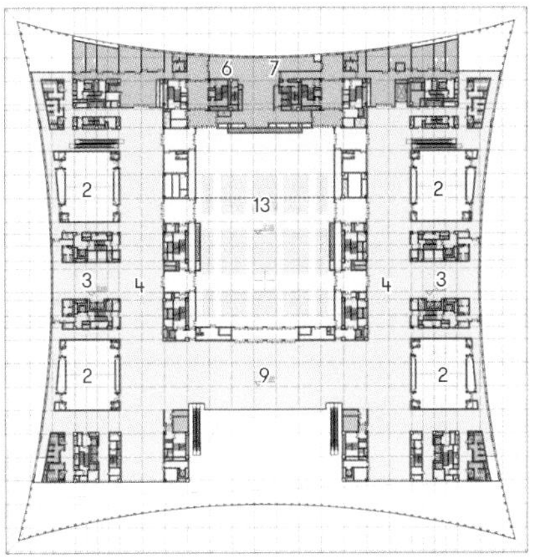

Third-floor plan

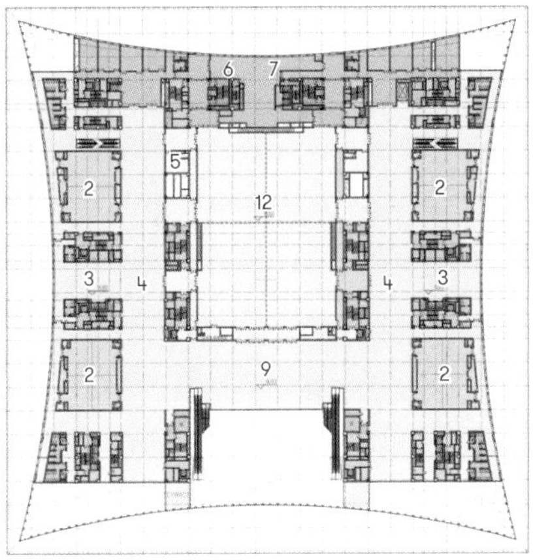

Second-floor plan

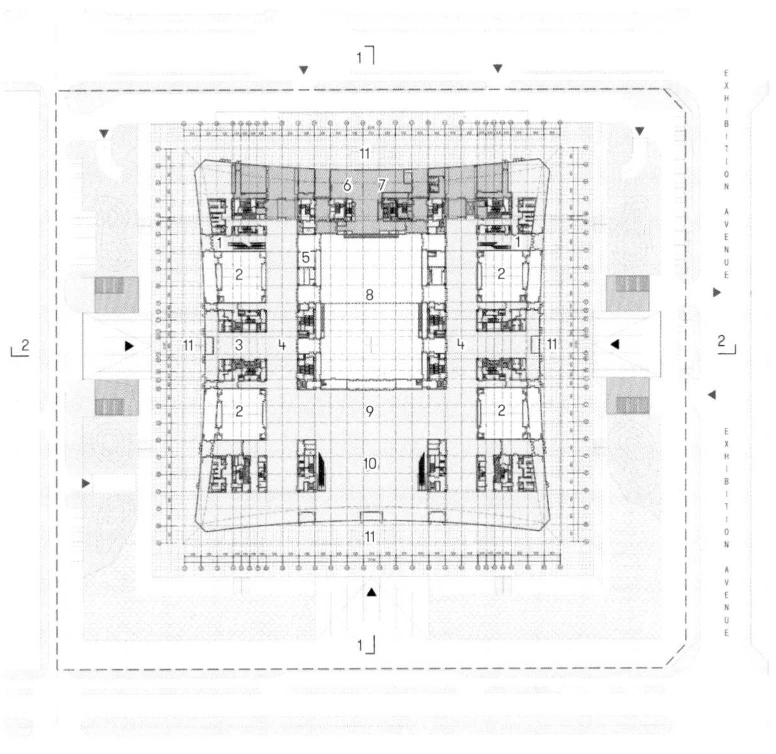

First-floor plan

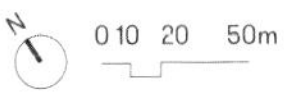

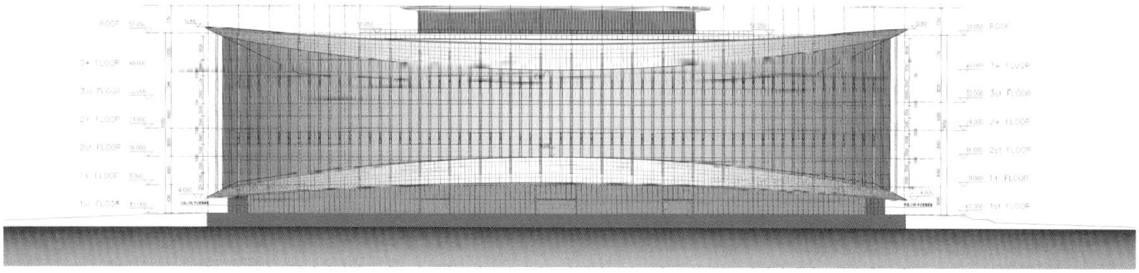

South elevation

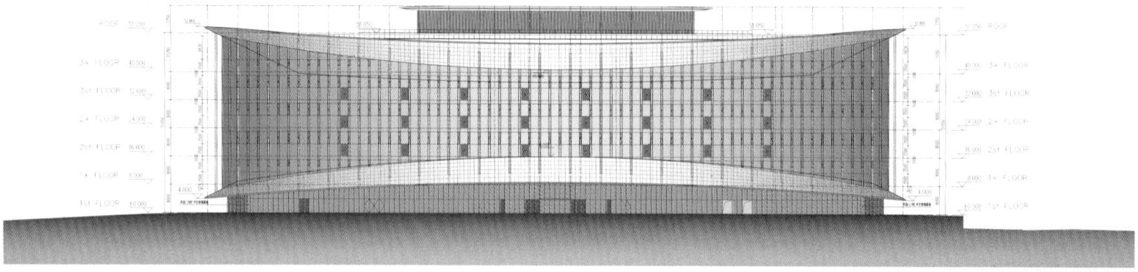

Elevations

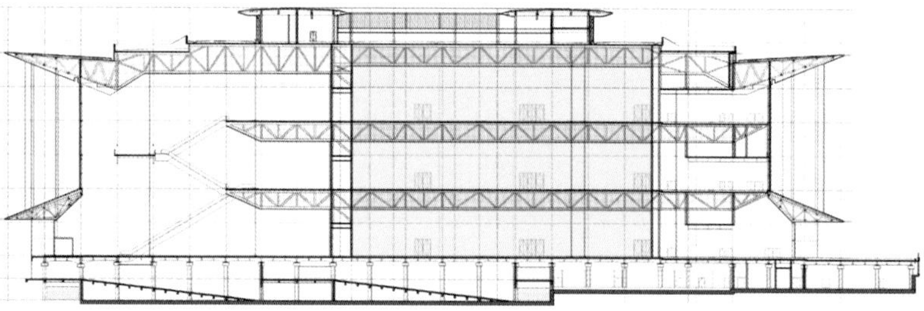

Section 1-1

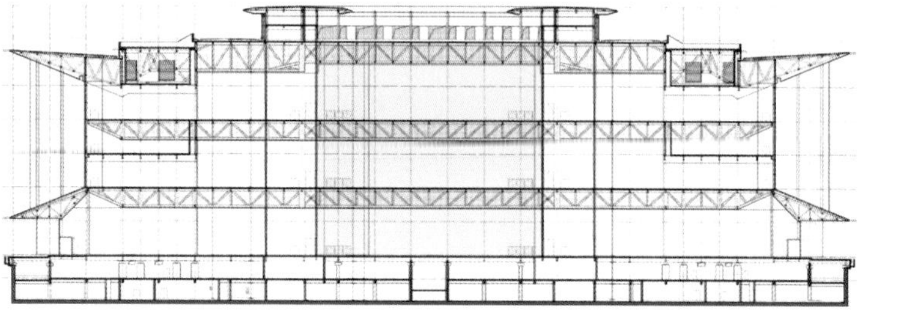

Section 2-2

Main conference hall

Multifunctional hall

Small conference hall

Reception and Administration Buildings of Yulin Grottoes

View of the office building from the opposite cliff

Architect firm: Nine Town Design Studio for Urban Architecture, China
Principal architect: HUANG Yinwu
Design team:
Architects – KE Chunjian, LIU Yong, YU Lei, GAO Wen, RANG Shanshan, SHAO Jie, LIAO Junyan
Structural engineers – ZHONG Jianmin, YANG Zhengyou, WU Yuying, ZHANG Zhenglei
Civil engineer – ZHONG Wenbin
M & E engineer – ZHOU Hao
Lighting engineer – HU Xin
Location: Guazhou, China
Area: 1,096.7 square meters
Completion date: August 2019
Photography: YAO Li

The Yulin Grottoes, known as the sister caves of the Mogao Grottoes in Dunhuang, are a collection of forty-two hand-carved caves that contain over 250 Buddhist statues and a staggering 4,200 square meters of colorful murals. The name "yulin" came about on account of the elm trees that line the riverbanks, creating a picturesque backdrop for the grottoes that punctuate the cliff faces on either bank.

The project is part of the overall program to upgrade the site's protection facilities, and is intended to prevent geological disasters, showcase the historical environment of the Yulin Grottoes, and better accommodate the site with the necessary functions of a "tourist spot," as well as the required administration facilities. To reduce the disturbance to the grottoes' environment, which is considered an integral part of the area's heritage, all unplanned previous constructions inside the protected area were demolished and all new constructions were allocated away from the cave area. To minimize the volume of each building, the new constructions include three buildings: a reception building, an office building with ticketing facilities, and a dormitory building with a canteen.

The reception building and office buildings, one near the top of the cliff and the other near the bottom, are located at the north end of the cave area where tourists start their visit. To reduce the visual impact of the building volume, the roof of the reception building is covered with earth, which helps to integrate the building volume into the cliff. A "slit" at the top of the building delineates a clear and non-optional access to the caves for tourists. The passageway that opens on one side of the reception building gives tourists the possibility to overlook the entire cave area and understand the heritage surroundings of the Yulin Grottoes.

The office building was conceived as a "bridge" over a gully. Under the building is a drainage channel for floods during the rainy season. Inside the building, is space for offices and ticket inspection. Above the building is an exit path for those who have finished their visit. Except for the exit path, the roof of the building is also covered with earth, as an extension of the cliffside slope, to reduce the visual impact of the building volume. The existing paper-burning tower serves as a visual connection between the reception building and the office building, so the buildings are well connected with the environment.

The dormitory building is located at the south end of the cave area, which few tourists will reach, and includes staff dormitories, a reading room, a canteen, and a kitchen. The building takes advantage of a small site that has been flattened on the cliffside slope and makes the building volume appear like a patch on the cliffside slope. The entrance to the building is formed in combination with the curved internal driveway, which also serves as a background for the original stupa.

The impact of the new constructions on the heritage site and its surrounding environment has been minimized by splitting the new buildings into smaller volumes and concealing the building volumes within the cliff, and also by using material textures similar to the cliff for exterior wall. At the same time, they also achieve the overall goal of providing more convenience to the function of heritage protection, tourist venue, and administration.

Bird's-eye view of the reception building and the office building

View of the office building from the steps

View from the dormitory entrance

View of the entrance of the dormitory

View of the office building from the platform

View of the reception building and office building from the passage connecting the caves

1. Reception
2. Management offices
3. Dormitory
4. Platform

Master plan

Bird's-eye view of the dormitory

View of the reception area from the valley

View from the gap between the management offices and the cliff

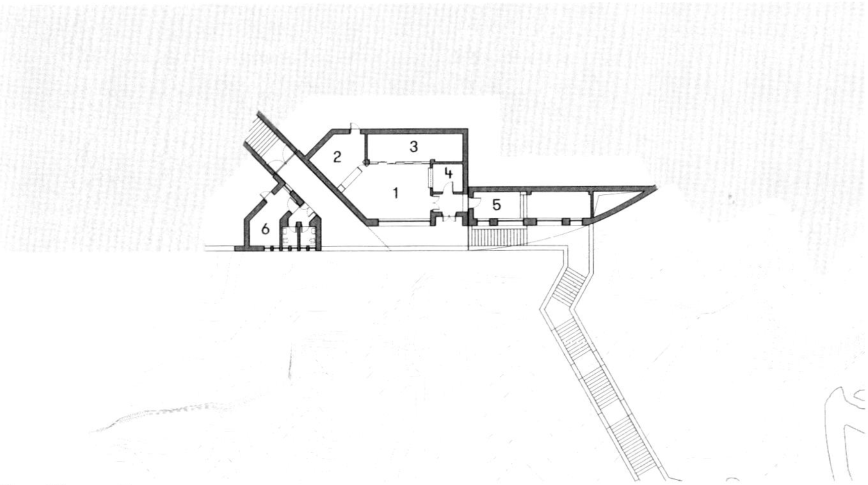

Plan of the reception

1. Entrance hall
2. Cloakroom
3. Gift shop
4. Ticket office
5. Archives
6. Guard house

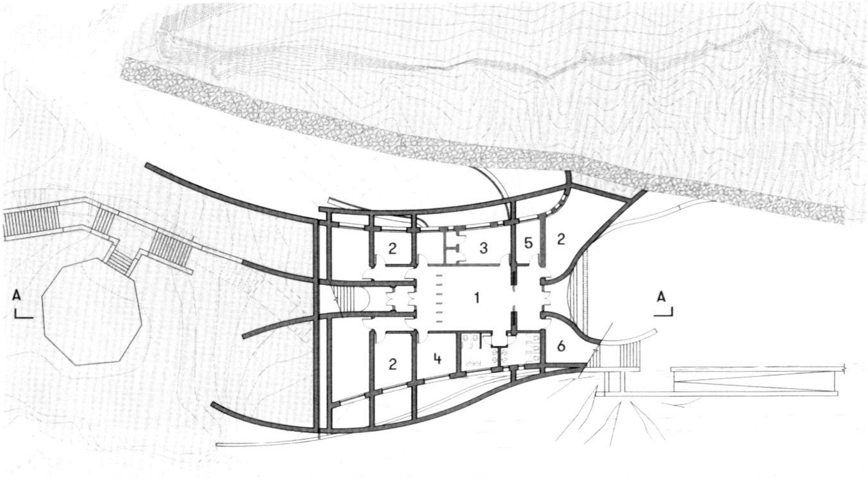

Plan of the office building

1. Entrance hall
2. Office
3. Docent lounge
4. Medical room
5. Guard house
6. Storage

Plan of the dormitory

1. Entrance hall
2. Canteen
3. Kitchen
4. Dormitory
5. Multifunction hall
6. Meeting room
7. Guard house
8. Courtyard

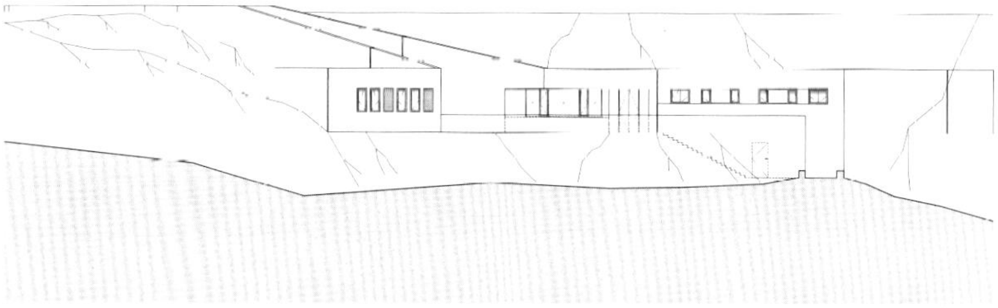

Elevation of the reception

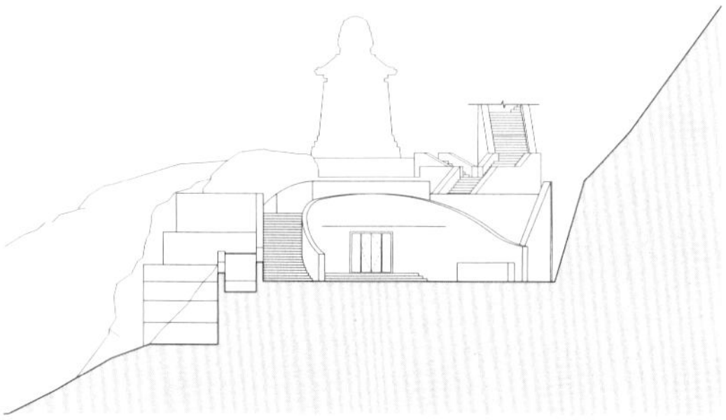

Elevation of the office building

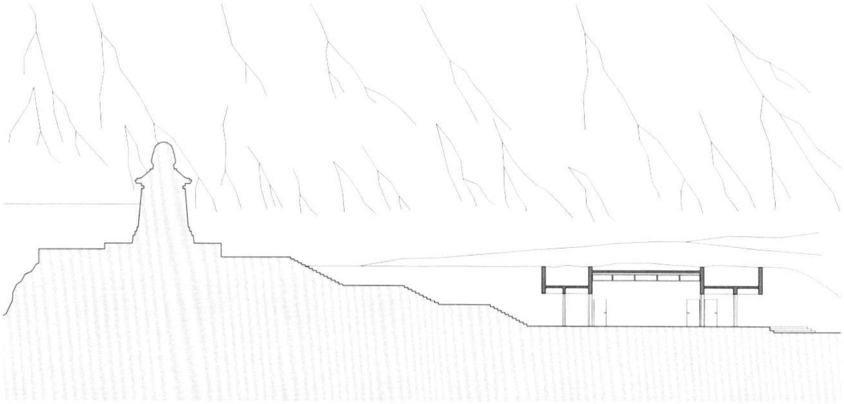

Section A

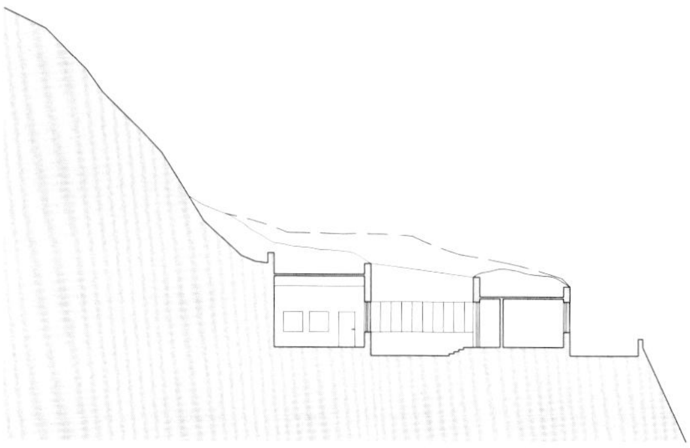

Section B

View of the reception area

View from the reception area

Jetavana, Somaiya Trust

Courtyard view toward the meditation hall

Architect firm: Sameep Padora & Associates (sP+a), India
Principal architect: Sameep PADORA
Design team: sP+a – Aparna DHARESHWAR, Kriti VEERAPAN, Karan BHAT
Hunnarshala – Kiran VAGHELA, Tejas KOTAK
Location: Sakarwadi, Maharashtra, India
Area: 1,858 square meters
Completion date: April 2016
Photography: Edmund SUMNER

In Buddhist mythology, Jetavana is one of the Buddha's most important spatial edifices; translated literally, it means "the grove of Jeta." This Jetavana project was an area of land donated to the sangha (the Buddhist monastic order) for the purposes of establishing a monastery. It is also symbolically significant that the site offered by Samir Somaiya, owner of the neighboring sugar factory in rural Maharashtra, for this Buddhist learning center is thickly forested, creating an idyllic grove of sorts, reminiscent of the famous Jetavana built in a park by Buddha's chief male patron, Anathapindika.

The institute is programed as a spiritual and skill development center for the native Dalit Baudh Ambedkar Buddhist community. The mandate of Jetavana is to provide a spiritual anchor for their practice of Buddhist thought through meditation and yoga, while also imparting training and skill development for members of the community.

Respecting and adhering to the mandate to not harm a single tree on-site, the sizable program is split into six buildings, each situated in gaps between the densely planted grove. Through the design process, two courtyards emerged as links suturing these buildings through common identity.

By inverting the roof profile to create a valley in the middle with lifted edges, the interior spaces are visually connected with the foliage outside. The interior spaces are, thus, also a function of the outside setting, with a lightness that belies the quantum of built program on-site. The separation of the roof from the walls—while providing much-needed cross ventilation—also scales the building toward the courtyard.

Working closely with Hunnarshala, an institution looking to revive and resuscitate local building traditions, the architects collated a material palate that uses rammed load-bearing walls of basalt stone dust. The stone dust, which is waste from a nearby quarry, is mixed with waste fly ash—a by-product from an adjoining factory that formerly used to pay people to cart the waste fly ash away. Repurposed wood from old shipping vessels act as the roof structure, with the understructure made of mud rolls, which also provide great insulation. The roof itself is finished with clay roof tiles, remnants from older demolished buildings. The flooring is a traditional mud-and-dung floor made by members of the local community, and is said to have antiseptic and insulating properties.

The approach to the Jetavana project looks to extend the idea of the regional paradigm while separating it from the pervasive "image" of what defines the local. The construction process also sets out an approach that looks to further construction techniques that are based on local materiality and which are appropriate to the context, even if they are not necessarily used natively.

Courtyard view toward Vocational Training hall

The butterfly-winged-roofs create an impression of opening to the sky as the courtyard is internalized; the basalt stone dust walls bring a tactility to the experience

Entry into the meditation hall from the arrival court

In-between the administration block and the two community hall spaces; repurposed PVC pipes are embedded within the rammed-stone-dust walls to create a porous screen

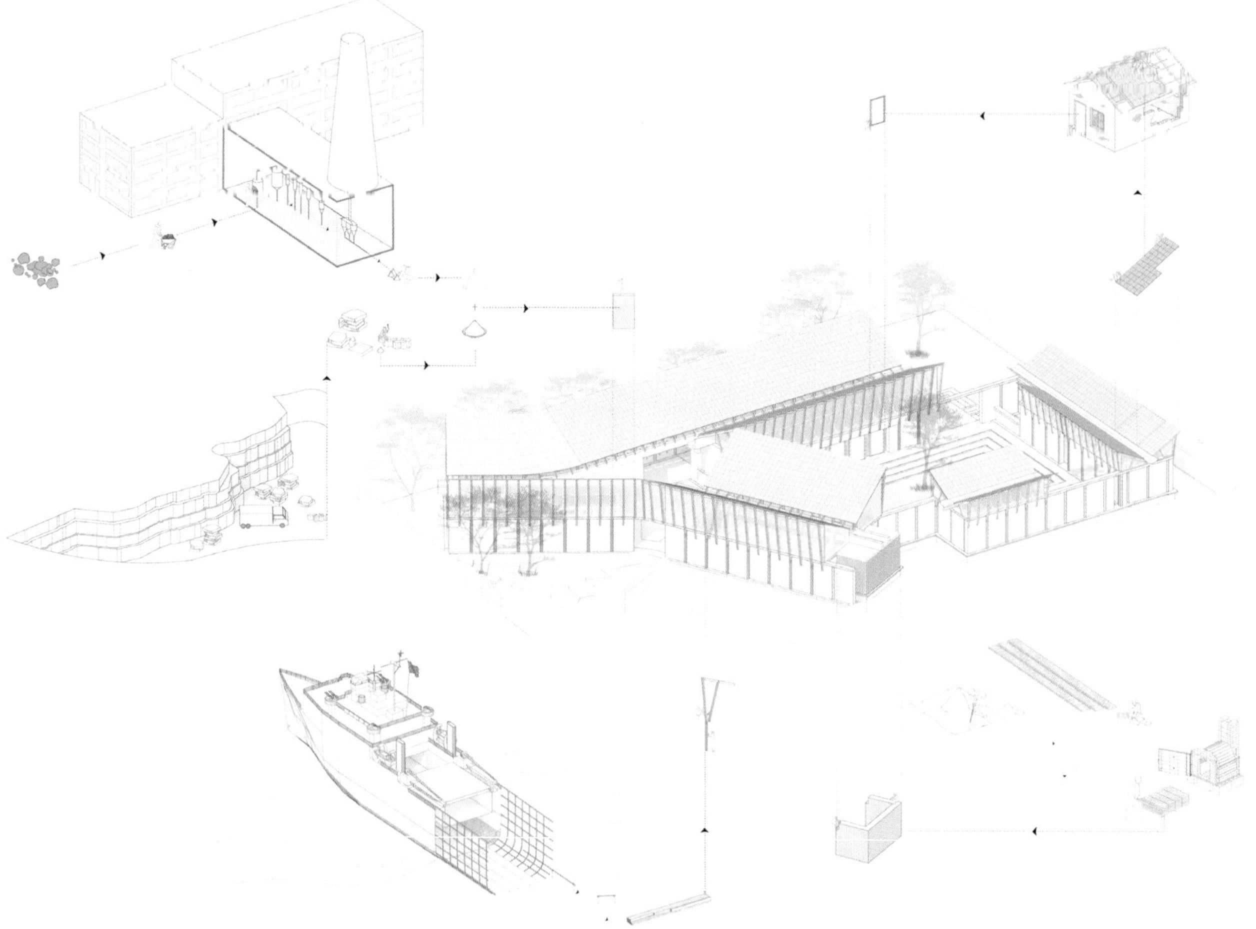

Materiality diagram

At the arrival court, which is structured around existing trees

Architecture as structure — recycled load-bearing brick alcoves

Inside the Vocational Training hall

Concept

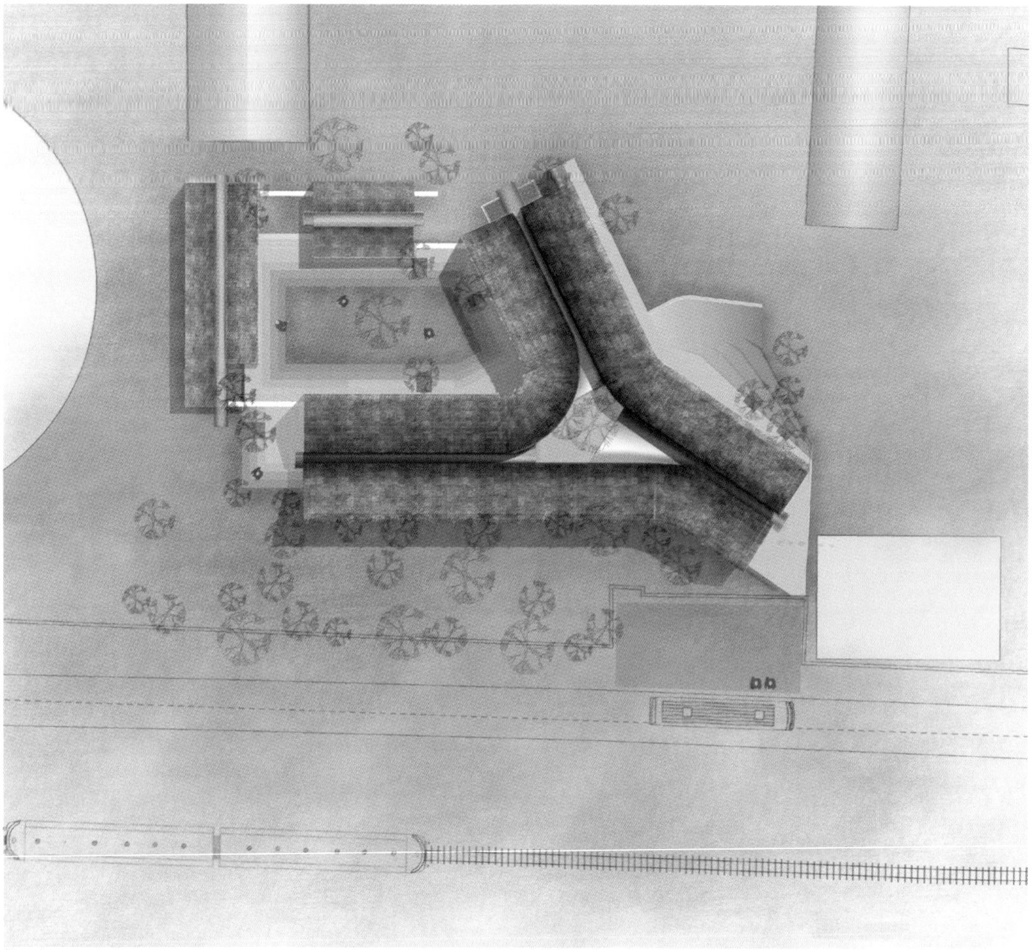

Site plan

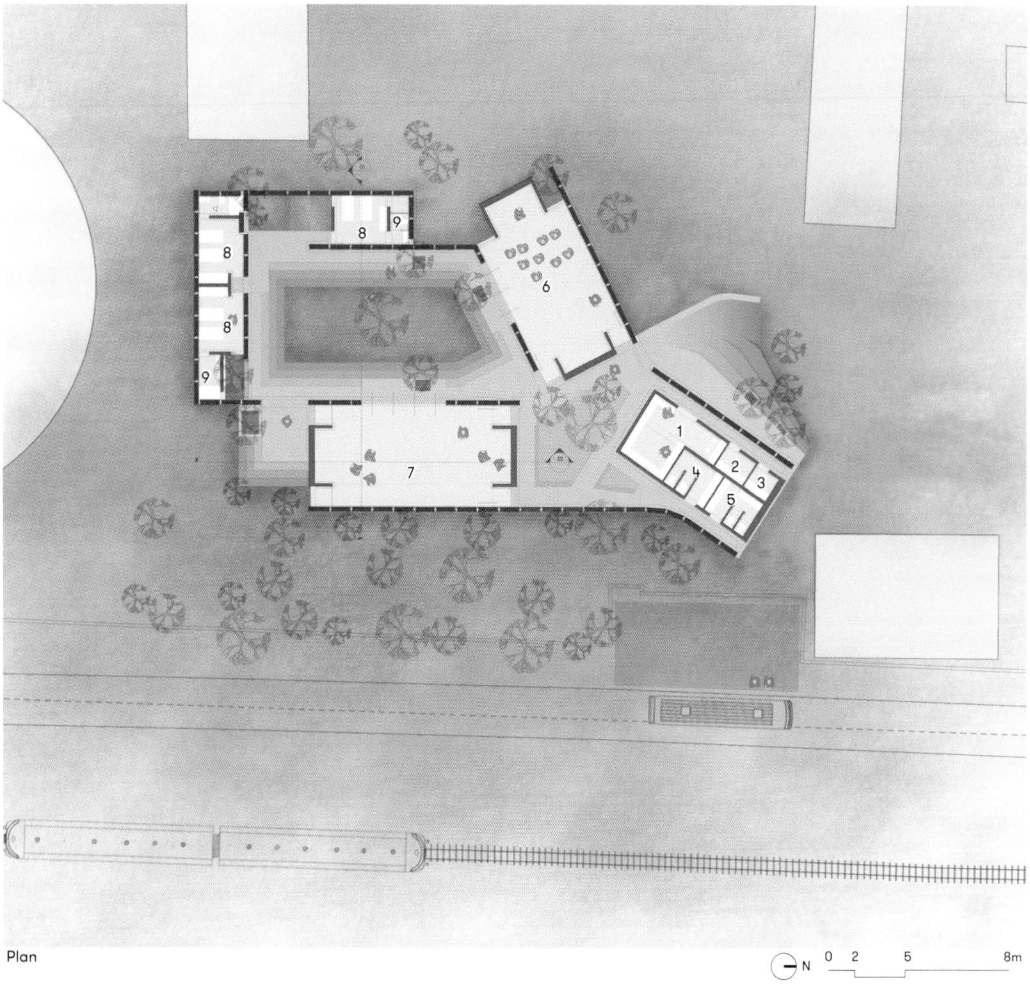

Plan

1. Administration office
2. Pantry
3. Storeroom
4. Men's restroom
5. Women's restroom
6. Prayer hall
7. Workshop block
8. Guestroom
9. Guest bathroom

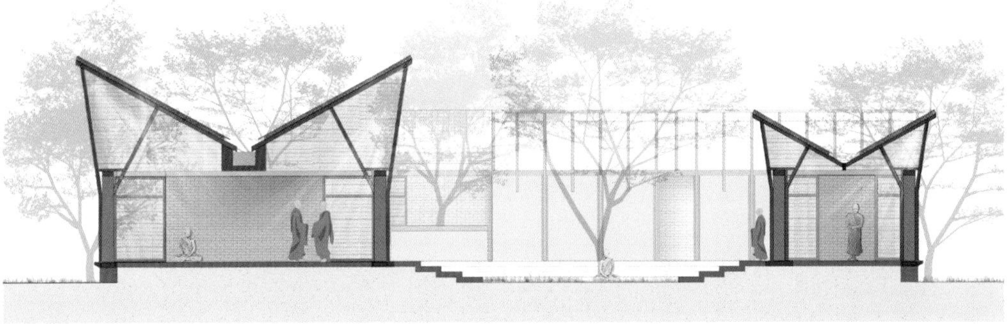

Section 1

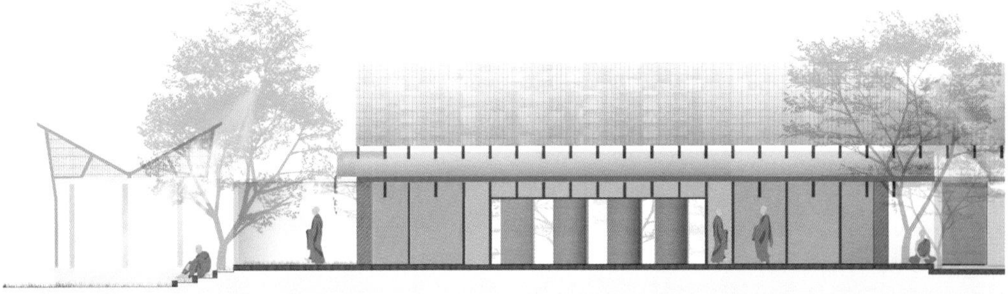

Section 2

0 1 2 3m

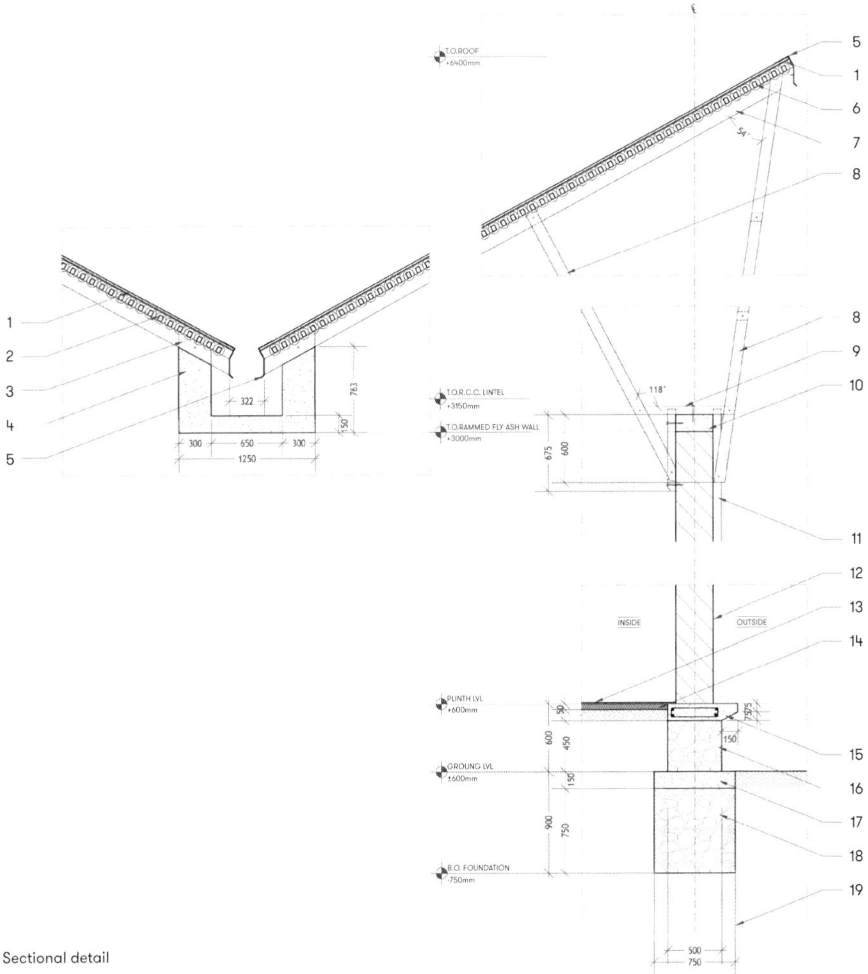

1. Reused mangalore tiles fixed on a wooden framework
2. Mud rolls
3. Wedge plates to anchor the rafter, 8mm thick
4. R.C.C. trough, ref. Str.dwgs
5. G.I. flashing
6. Mud rolls, 100mmØ, 600mm long
7. Reused tw rafter, 38mm x 127mm size @ 830mm c/c
8. 2 nos. of reused tw member, 38mm x 100mm size @ 830mm c/c
9. Reused tw member, 50mm x 75mm size @ 830mm c/c
10. R.C.C. lintel, 150mm thick
11. Reused tw rafter, 75mm x 127mm size @ 830mm c/c
12. Rammed-stone-dust wall, 345mm thick
13. Mud+cow dung plaster, 12mm thick
14. Rammed-earth layer, 50mm thick
15. R.C.C plinth band, 150mm thick
16. UCR masonry with 1:6 mortar mix, 500mm thick
17. P.C.C (1:3:6), Re.Str.dwgs
18. UCR masonry foundation
19. Soling

Sectional detail

Zis[illegible]ion and Pla[illegible]

View at dusk © Chao Zhang

Architect firm: Mozhao Architects, China
Principal architect: ZENG Guansheng
Design team: LUO Wenguo, SHEN Jiayuan, HONG Fenglian, CHEN Xun
Location: Shenzhen, China
Area: 2,080 square meters
Completion date: May 2016
Photography: ZHANG Chao

With the advantage of a favorable geographical location, Shajing in Shenzhen has managed to largely develop its low-end manufacturing industry over the last two to three decades. However, the mass construction of factories not only destroyed the scenic wetlands and farmlands, but also brought chaos to the nearby suburbs, and the industrial parks and external urban spaces began to be perceived as negative places.

In recent years, many residential buildings and schools have been built around the industrial park. This project hopes to provide a dynamic public space for workers, residents, teachers, students, and nature lovers by reshaping a green space for humanity.

In the original site layout, there was an outdoor parking lot in the west next to the courtyard. In order to meet the demand for parking and to improve the spatial quality of the courtyard, a large landscaped terrace that covers the parking lot is created. Connected by steps, this large terrace becomes an extension of the courtyard through which the courtyard establishes a public space system on different levels. The steps also serve as seats for the audience when outdoor activities are held in the courtyard.

Concrete planting troughs are placed randomly on the terrace, where people can plant various crops and shrubs, depending on their individual preferences, so that these crops and shrubs create an interesting and vivid landscape. The big "hole" on the terrace provides better sunlight for the parking lot below and the camphor tree in the middle of the "hole" also provides shade for parked vehicles.

With various experiential activities held in the space, the traditional planting culture of Shajing is passed down in a new form, which is also a medium for community building.

At the same time, in the northeast of the terrace, there is a planting pavilion made of exposed concrete, which brings greenery fans together to learn from one another. The first floor is a public space for exhibitions, communications, and lectures, while the second floor is intended as a planting and training space. The two-story-high green vegetation wall exhibits various plants, while the two-story-high space becomes a place of learning and communication, where people can chat, exchange notes, and interact with each other.

The cantilevered staircase and the hanging floor in the building make the structure's form appear light and delicate. At the same time, the two entrances on different levels of the building create a closer connection between the terrace, the interior space, and the courtyard.

The parking lot before renovation © Chao Zhang

Different kinds of activities © Chao Zhang

The planting terrace at sunset © Chao Zhang

Children running on the terrace © Chao Zhang

Plan of the planting terrace

1. Wooden platform
2. Concrete flower bed
3. Wooden seat
4. Wooden stairs

Bird's-eye view © Chao Zhang

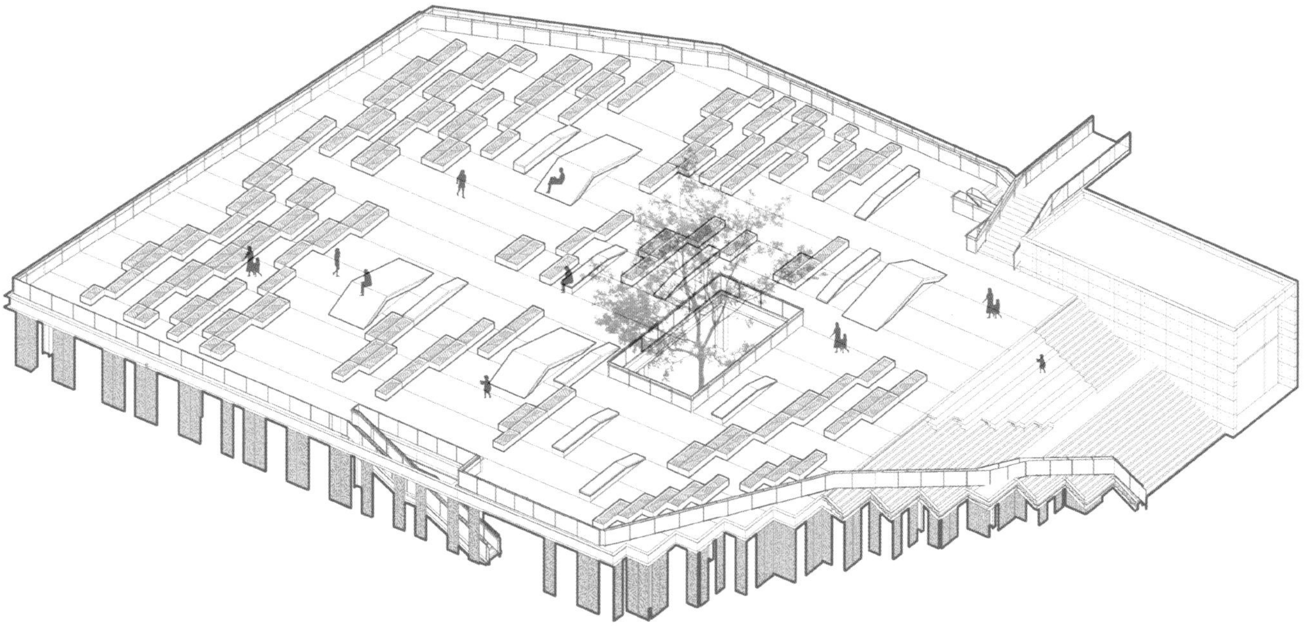

Axonometric drawing of the planting terrace

The terrace as a green and dynamic space © Chao Zhang

Children playing in the garden © Chao Zhang

A casual and joyful scene of people-interaction in the experience pavilion © Chao Zhang

The bench space as a playground © Chao Zhang

Section

Night view of the experience pavilion © Chao Zhang

1. Experience hall
2. Storage
3. Toolshed
4. Seedling cultivation room

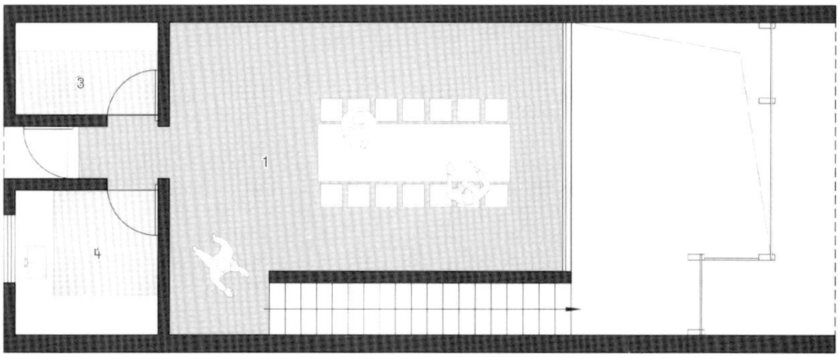

Second-floor plan

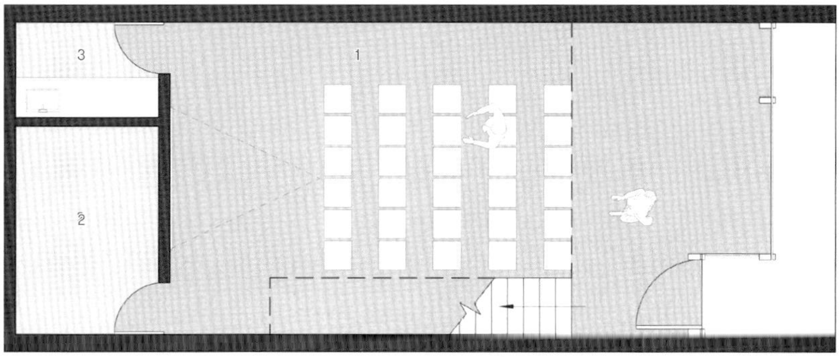

First-floor plan

The interior cantilevered staircase © Chao Zhang

The experience pavilion made of exposed concrete © Chao Zhang

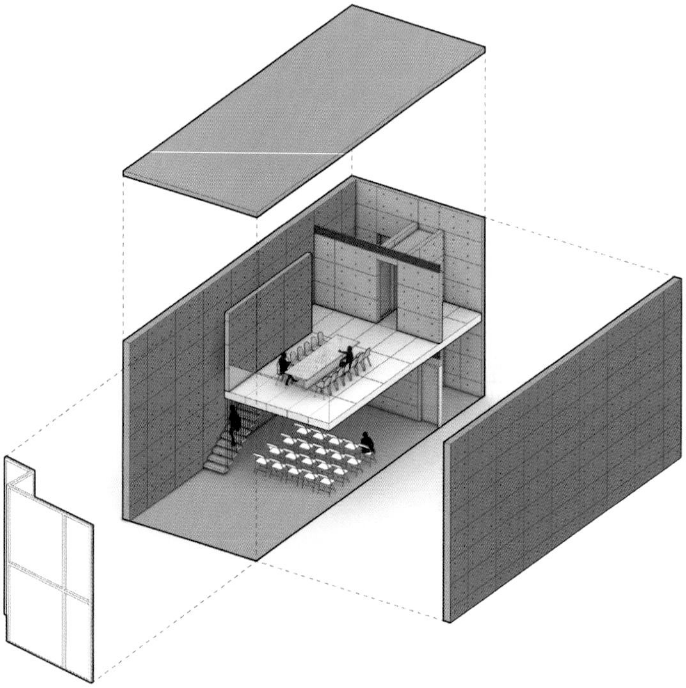
Exploded drawing of the experience pavilion

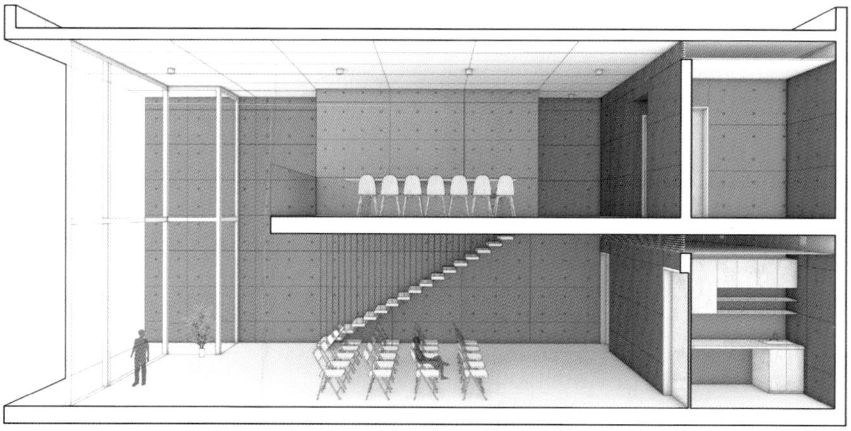
Perspective section of the experience pavilion